POSTSCRIPTS
A few final tips

Beware of lyrics   145
Blake Morrison, author of And When Did You
Last See Your Father?

Get a deadline   149
Guardian *columnist Charlie Brooker*

Love your stationery   153
Hilary Mantel, author of Wolf Hall

BEFORE you BEGIN

INTRODUCTION

CLAIRE ARMITSTEAD,
GUARDIAN LITERARY EDITOR

It's a truth worth acknowledging that more people think they have a book in them than ever get round to writing it. Prevarication is part of life even for those writers who do manage to get published – so what is it that distinguishes them from the rest of us, and what tips can they offer?

A useful first step towards beating the block is to break it down into its constituent parts: time is short, life is distracting. Well yes, but look behind those apparently insurmountable obstacles and a more traversible landscape begins to emerge. How do you begin? How do you develop a voice? How do you create character, or plot or suspense? These are among the subjects tackled in this book by the distinguished line-up of writers who have taught at our *Guardian* Masterclasses.

The old saw "do what I do, not what I say" has a particular resonance for the aspiring author. As both a writer and an editor, I'm forever quoting to myself rule 5 from Neil Gaiman: "Remember: when people tell you something's wrong or doesn't work for them, they are almost always right. When they tell you exactly what they think is wrong and how to fix it, they are almost always wrong." All too frequently, after a long day wrestling with myself, I gratefully succumb to Helen Dunmore's rule 3: "Read Keats' letters".

One of the best tips for any writer is to find a community of other like-minded people to support and nourish you. We have gathered our own literary community of contributors to *Guardian Review*, to share some of their hard-won wisdom.

Exchanging stories helps, as Jonathan Franzen discovered when writing *The Corrections*. A conversation with a fellow writer, David Means, produced the insight: "You don't write through shame, you write around it". Even though he didn't quite understand what it meant at the time, Franzen followed the advice. His creative block dissolved and one of his finest characters, Chip Lambert, was born.

We hope the insights collected in this book will inspire you, too, to beat the block and liberate your inner writer.

HOW
to
WRITE

THE FUNDAMENTALS OF FICTION

GETTING STARTED

JILL DAWSON, AUTHOR OF *FRED & EDIE*

Nabokov called it 'the first little throb'. The first inkling of the novel you want to write. He was speaking of *Lolita*, of course. Something that beats beneath everything else; something troubling, insistent, itchy and physical: pain and desire mixed. In his earlier novella *The Enchanter*, which feels in some ways like an early draft of *Lolita*, the protagonist speaks of his 'hopeless yearning to extract something from beauty, to hold it still for an instant, to do something with it'.

Maybe that's what the desire to write a novel is. Trying to hold something still, pin it down, stick things (words) to paper. Maybe . . . but plenty of writers, and I'm definitely in this group, couldn't tell you at the start why they wanted to write a particular novel, only that they feel this throb powerfully.

I urge new writers to dive in. There is never a perfect time to write your novel, though writing students seem to believe there is. Begin today. That has been my consistent advice in the 20 or so years I've been writing, or teaching writing, or talking about writing.

I can, of course, see the temptations of not beginning. Chiefly, not beginning sustains the belief that you are gifted, that the novel – when you one day get round to writing it – will surpass all others, that you will suffer no rejections, that it will be published at once and be thereafter visible in every bookshop you step into, that you will never suffer a bad review or sit at a dinner party and hear the question: 'So, should I have heard of you?'

Not beginning protects you from the disappointment – no, shame – of reading what you have written and finding it rubbish. It also prevents you from an equally disturbing possibility: discovering that you can write. What then have you been doing all those years? Success or failure can both be avoided by never starting at all – this then is the spell that procrastination casts. How to step out from under it?

The writers I know are all obsessive. The unpublished ones obsess over getting published; the rest about 'this crazy obsessive business of trying to be a good writer' (in the words of American novelist Richard Yates). You could try to put this compulsive trait to good use. Yes, you might need to start with some research, but you don't have to spend years on this before feeling ready to begin. You can also research alongside the writing, making the most of your obsessive qualities, which will keep the material fresh and give you something to do on the days when writing doesn't go well. While writing *The Great Lover* I reread the poems and letters of Rupert Brooke over and over, which did indeed change the structure of the novel (I'd never intended to include Brooke's voice). Surprise in fiction can be a pleasure for you as well as the reader. And conversely, if you're bored, your reader will be too.

Shouldn't you complete the research, plot it out, know where it's going before you put finger to key? I know there are writers who work this way, but not being one of them, I can't tell you about that method. It might suit you. But so might mine.

There is much anxiety created in new writers about writing the beginning of their novel, how the first line has to grab the reader's attention, how they must open with a vivid scene or phrase, that kind of thing. Reading wonderful opening lines makes it look easy and implies that there is a formula for this – shock the reader by opening with: 'Mother died today, or maybe yesterday, I don't know' (Camus's *The Outsider*), or stun them with lyrical virtuosity: 'Lolita, light of my life, fire of my loins. My sin, my soul. Lo-lee-ta: the tip of the tongue taking a trip of three steps down the palate to tap, at three, on the teeth. Lo. Lee. Ta.'

Brilliant opening lines rarely come to the writer the minute she or he begins, so why worry, especially since it's much easier now than in Nabokov's day to make changes to a manuscript? The perfect opener is more likely to suggest itself after you have many more words on paper, once you know the characters well, once the whole thing feels thicker and juicier and more developed.

Whatever your level of experience, writing a novel usually feels like a series of false starts. When we begin the voice sounds wrong, the characters don't 'come through', the tone is wrong, even the year and the place you've put them in feel wrong. But how can you, the writer, know these things, see them, until you've put words on the page, taken a look at them? This is drafting. Resisting producing a draft means not producing anything at all ('Perfection is terrible . . . it tamps the womb,' wrote Plath). Is the prose alive or dead? That's all you need to know to carry on.

Most draft novels, like old bread, would benefit from topping and tailing. But you can't do that until there's something solid, some dry crusts to slice away. A rough start is unavoidable, a warm-up. There's no way to write a novel without being willing to do this.

The trick is not to care that it all gets pared away, not to mourn those thousands of abandoned words, those endless new beginnings. Weak beginnings are inevitable and essential. The first little throb turns into a steady pulse, a heartbeat, the tapping of keys. It's an austere and repetitive service, the writing of a novel. But, of course, there is joy too.

CREATING CHARACTERS

ANDREW MILLER, AUTHOR OF *OXYGEN*

First, a note of caution. To slice up fiction into categories such as 'plot', 'voice', 'point of view', 'characterisation', is to risk presenting it in a way that neither writer nor reader normally experiences it. The suggestion might seem to be that the writing of a story or a novel is a strongly segmented or layered activity, something orderly, dry and technical. But stories when they come, come in bloody organic gobs, as though gouged out of the living fabric of the world – character tangled with plot, plot with setting, setting with scraps of language embedded, and so on. But laying that aside, that large proviso, there are, I suppose, a few remarks that might be usefully attempted under the heading of 'characterisation'.

First off (and at the risk of being punched in the face by some elderly follower of the Nouveau Roman school) let it be loudly asserted that character, strong characters, are at the heart of all great literature and always will be. Plot, even in detective fiction, is a very secondary matter. Not many readers could outline the plot of The Sign of the Four but no one has any difficulty bringing Holmes and Watson to mind. A writer who does not create convincing characters will fail. A writer who creates thrilling, troubling, seductive, insistent characters, need not worry too much about any other aspect of writing. You do not need to know how to spell. You do not need to know much about grammar. You do not even need any huge sensitivity to language, though your case will be vastly strengthened if you do possess it. Sensitivity to language is the other quality that really matters in writing; it is also, perhaps, the most resistant to any kind of formal teaching.

So having insisted, so immoderately, on the central importance of character, how, in God's name, is it done? Luckily, the raw material is close to hand. For every writer it is his own enigmatic being that constitutes the focus of his researches. Year after year he sits on a kind of umpire's chair, watching the antics of his body, listening to the bubbling of his thoughts, sifting the material of his dreams. And when he wants more – other bodies, other thoughts – he simply looks up at those around him. Think, for a moment, of your own family. Almost everybody has one. You might never need to go beyond them. You could keep them all in a kind of mental aquarium, sketch them into stories all your writing life. Change their names, of course, their hair colour, their tattoos, move them from that little town in the South you grew up in to a little town in the North you once drove through and wondered about...

But a writer is not confined to such a tactic. It may even be that such a tactic is not particularly common. In my own work I have very rarely set out to present a character who is knowingly and intentionally based on someone familiar to me, someone whose name I might find in an address book. The great majority of my characters – and I would guess this is true for most writers of fiction – are 'inventions'. They emerge, quickly or slowly, shyly or boisterously, in the writing. They are members of that shifting population of men, women and children (not to mention cats, horses etc) who inhabit our inner worlds. Where they come from, whether they are curious versions of ourselves, figures out of the collective unconscious, reconfigurings of those we did indeed once know but have now forgotten, or a mix of all such, no one, to my knowledge, has ever convincingly answered. It does not matter. No one writes for long without understanding that they are entering mystery and will never leave it. What matters is that we can, from unnamed processes, secrete these figures who will loom and mouth-off in our fictions. It is not, I think, too much to say that it is a 'natural' process, that we are, all of us, geared up for it, and that without this propensity all of writing would be impossibly complex. We could not do it.

There is, of course, another great resevoir of characters: those ready-made for us in books. It is not that we intend to steal Mr Tulkinghorn from Dickens or Ursula Brangwen from Lawrence, but that such characters show us the dimensions of the possible. A painter who wants to paint a tree needs to do two things: look at trees and look at paintings of trees. The first activity tells her what trees are like, the second tells her about the possibilities of her medium. Likewise, as a writer it is by reading that you learn how, in language, a character can be presented – through dialogue, through action, through physical attributes, interior monologue etc – a process that continues until you have absorbed these methods, these possibilities, and they have become a reflex so embedded in your apprehending of the world that you will never notice anything about anybody without secretly assessing its potential for fiction, for writing. And this, indeed, we could call 'technique', though we should not confuse the method with the task. At its simplest, its barest, characterisation is about a writer's grasp of what a human being is. When we set out to write we do not do so out of a sense of *certainty* but out of a kind of radical uncertainty. We do not set out saying, 'The world is like this' but asking, 'How is the world?'. In creating characters we are posing to ourselves large, honest questions about our nature and the nature of those about us. Our answers are the characters themselves, those talking spirits we have conjured up by a kind of organised dreaming. And when we finish we will immediately begin to be dissatisfied with them, these 'answers', and we will set out again, bemused, frustrated, excited. An odd use of time. An odd use of a life. But there's a courage to it. Even, perhaps, a type of beauty.

...✒

FINDING YOUR VOICE

MEG ROSOFF, AUTHOR OF *HOW I LIVE NOW*

Do you have a voice? Can you recognise a voice when you hear one? And while we're on the subject, what does 'having a voice' actually mean?

Poetry is a great place to look for a strong voice. How about:

How to Kill a Living Thing

Neglect it
Criticise it to its face
Say how it kills the light
Traps all the rubbish
Bores you with its green

Continually
Harden your heart
Then
Cut it down close
To the root as possible

Forget it
For a week or a month
Return with an axe
Split it with one blow
Insert a stone

To keep the wound wide open

Do you hear a voice in those lines? Although I am unable to pronounce her name, the author Eibhlin Nic Eochaidh's voice is so clear to me, I'm tempted to offer her a chair and a cup of tea.

Many would-be writers spend far too much time nervously scrabbling about for a voice, but the word itself is horribly misleading. 'Voice' (unlike 'power', for instance, or 'presence') suggests a superficial quality, one that can be manipulated by having singing lessons, or by changing the tone, volume or accent.

There is nothing superficial, however, about voice when used in the context of writing. Your writing voice is the deepest possible reflection of who you are. The job of your voice is not to seduce or flatter or make well-shaped sentences. In your voice, your readers should be able to hear the contents of your mind, your heart, your soul.

So. . . what is the essence of your personality? What is the clearest expression of your DNA combined with a lifetime of experience? What does the combination of nature and nurture add up to? In other words, who are you? Who are you really?

If you don't know, you need to find out. Self-knowledge is essential not only to writing, but to doing almost anything really well. It allows you to work through from a deep place – from the deep, dark corners of your subconscious mind. This connection of subconscious to conscious mind is what gives a writer's voice resonance.

Read a great writer and you'll feel the resonance – it's the added dimension of power that can't quite be explained by mere talent. An ability with words is nice, but it's not a voice.

Connecting with your subconscious mind is not easy. It requires confronting difficult facts – about yourself and about the world. Can you know who you are without understanding your own weaknesses? And what frightens you? Can you know who you are without understanding the evil, the selfishness, the cruelty of which you're capable? OK. And the goodness, kindness, brilliance as well?

Of course the biggest, darkest question of all is death. Not an easy question to meet head-on. Some people naturally confront death. Some seem incapable of confronting it. Woody Allen says that when he was a small child he lay in bed, terrified, contemplating eternal nothingness. So, apparently, did William Golding. Many people, however, live their lives in evasion of the central fact of existence.

Of course it is perfectly possible to be a writer without facing death face-on, without years of psychoanalysis, and without a tendency towards depression. But the resonant, powerful, exciting voice that grips you in its thrall is likely to be a voice with a good deal of hard-won wisdom about humanity.

Which brings us to 'throughness'. 'Throughness' is a word I've borrowed from dressage: 'the supple, elastic, unblocked, connected state that permits an unrestricted flow of energy from back to front and front to back'. Synonymous with the German term

Durchlässigkeit or 'throughlettingness', it is often used in conjunction with the word 'connection' – defined as a state 'in which there is no blockage, break, or slack in the circuit that joins horse and rider into a single harmonious unit; the unrestricted flow of energy and influence from and through the rider to and throughout the horse, and back to the rider'.

Now think, for a minute, of your subconscious mind as the horse and your conscious mind as the rider. The goal is a combination of strength, suppleness and softness. If the rider (conscious mind) is too strong, too stiff or unsympathetic, the horse becomes unresponsive and difficult to control, or resistant and dull.

The object of dressage is to create an open, graceful exchange of understanding and energy between horse and rider. In writing, a powerful flow of energy between conscious and subconscious mind will result in extraordinary occurrences. Characters will behave in ways you had not anticipated. Twists of plot will astound you. The part of your brain that concocts elaborate dreams while you sleep will emerge in daytime, informing your story in ways you might never have anticipated.

A book written with an exchange of energy between the conscious and subconscious mind will feel exciting and fluid in the way that a perfectly planned and pre-plotted book never will. Writing (like riding, or singing, or playing a musical instrument, or painting or playing cricket or thinking about the universe) requires the deep psychological resonance of the subconscious mind. It requires throughness and connection, and only then will the reader feel the surge of power that a clever borrowed voice never achieves.

The good news is that you can achieve throughness by writing. Practice, in other words. Write first thing in the morning when your conscious brain hasn't quite taken over yet. Write letters. Or essays. Write and write and write, and then look at what you've written to find out who you are.

Last bit of advice? Stop thinking about your voice. Think about your life instead. Live. Take risks. Seek wisdom. Confront the unconfrontable. Find out who you are. Let your voice gain power as you go.

Then write your book.

CONVINCING DIALOGUE

DBC PIERRE, AUTHOR OF *VERNON GOD LITTLE*

What characters say to each other in a book will make or break it. Their dialogues not only move the story along, mask and unveil truth, slow or quicken pace, cause or dampen conflict; they make the work credible or incredible.

And as if that doesn't already sound hard enough – they must also make us forget we're reading them.

A few basic laws govern dialogue and, once applied, their effect will be immediate. If you're beginning to make your characters speak, I promise these basics will help.

UNNATURAL IS NATURAL

Our programming as listeners and readers creates a need for technique in dialogue; these are two different things, as you'll discover when you try to write what you hear. At first I couldn't understand why the conversations around me wouldn't translate verbatim to a page; but a refraction effect applies – sentences strangely bend, like light hitting water. The first law then: natural speech looks unnatural when written.

Record someone's speech and you'll hear how peppered with reversals, repetitions and omissions it is. In its quest for meaning, the brain filters these out, delivering us a clean, packaged concept, which is great – until you try to write it. The way around this is concision. As an exercise, start with the dialogue you want to write, then remove every third word, or cut the sentence by half; cut it until the meaning no longer survives, then add back the few words that return the meaning you want.

You'll be surprised by how few words a sentence needs to do its job. Readers will fly through dialogue – it's one of the great pleasures of reading and one that puts them at the heart of the action. Don't slow or stop them, except by design. Tight dialogue may look curt at first, but let it rest overnight then look again; you'll see that in the reading brain, economy is natural.

SHOW, DON'T TELL

You might be sick of this catchphrase, but it's a rule that applies particularly to dialogue, as this is where you will show things rather than tell them. Where it might be easier to describe an action or setting in prose, the reader will become more involved in your work if your characters expose things through dialogue and action. For instance, this might be an interesting piece of prose:

Then there was Barry, wearing his usual sour face. Rather than complain of the cold, or put on a jumper, he had a habit of drowning his food in salt, as he said this stimulated the body's temperature-regulating mechanisms. Of course it was because he simply liked salt but was ashamed to admit it after warnings he'd received about his health. Still, he usually froze at dinner to prop up this facade.

Now note how engaged we become when we see the tale unfold through dialogue. This exchange says all the same things:

'Pass the salt,' said Barry. Mother frowned at this and he didn't meet her gaze. 'Not a crime, is it?' he mumbled, 'a bit of salt? Against the cold?'

'If I thought it'd cheer you up I might pass it,' she said. 'Or you could just get a jumper like the rest of us.'

'They say chillies regulate body temperature,' chimed Silvia. 'And tea.'

Dan finished a mouthful, leaning back: 'Tea regulates by making you sweat. He's hardly going to sweat. Lucky if he's any fluids left, I've filled the shaker twice already.'

'Not a crime, is it?'

'Ask Doctor Brice. Ask him after you've popped a vein.'

BEAT AROUND THE BUSH

One element of spoken dialogue that we aim to preserve is indirectness. If you listen to how we speak you'll note much of what we say assumes that we know each other.

More than this, much of our speech is just a cover – for barbs, for questions, for things we don't want to deal with directly.

This is all good in writing. It draws readers in because it not only seems natural, but makes them eavesdroppers. It gives mysteries to unravel, suspicions to confirm, which are as rewarding in books as in life. Your character Richard, for instance, in life or in a book, would never come out and say: 'Nell, I hold you and your absences responsible for the pressures on our marriage.' Instead, we would guess it from an exchange like this:

Nell clattered downstairs: 'I might be late home.'
'Could've sworn I left it around here.'
'Feel free to ignore me.'
'Works well enough for you.'

LET IT FLOW

Flowing dialogue has to be balanced with letting readers know which character is speaking; but dialogue with too many 'he said's and 'she said's is irritating. It's a perennial challenge to clearly identify who's speaking without lumbering the exchange with repetitious words. While the beginning of a dialogue should firmly show who speaks and who answers, if the conversation continues you will need some new tools to keep it natural, unobtrusive and rhythmic.

One of a new writer's first responses can be to substitute other verbs for 'said'. While you can get away with a certain number of basic substitutions, they quickly wear thin. There are more elegant ways to identify your speakers.

First, don't put all your attributions at the end – try breaking sentences with them:

> 'By the time I left the pub I could barely see them,' said Richard.
> 'By the time I left the pub,' said Richard, 'I could barely see them.'

Try shifting attributions around to find where they fit best. Better still, attribute with action; take the opportunity to show what Richard is doing as he speaks:

> 'By the time I left the pub,' Richard lifted the blind: 'I could barely see them.'

TAG YOUR VOICES

Perhaps the sharpest tool in the armoury, one that removes attributions altogether, is the speech tag – this is one of the grunts or tics we agreed to eliminate at the beginning. Across the length of a story readers come to know a character by the style of their speech, by idiosyncrasies. Everyone has their habits, whether beginning replies with 'Hmm' or 'But' or 'Well', pronouncing things a certain way, or having a characteristic pause.

The key here is to pick one or two for each main character, and lead their sentences with them. Don't overuse these tags: wait until you're at full stretch to attribute dialogues – but then, with a tag each, your characters can chat at some length without needing to pause for a 'said Richard'.

Don't worry if the tags seem awkward at first – add them to mark for yourself who's speaking; they'll develop and become more subtle as your characters settle into themselves.

Few tools in writing have such immediate effect on the page as these do, fuelling confidence, boosting the work along. We live in the best time for dialogue-heavy books – because it's fast, and we're fast, and it makes us eavesdroppers and ticks commercial boxes if you want to be published. Pace sells and dialogue is pace; you can still make unique, compelling characters, and you can still write a unique work around them – but a reader who falls into good dialogue on the first page of a book is in your pocket.

'Treat him bloody well,' said Richard.

DESCRIPTION
WITH MEANING

ADAM FOULDS, AUTHOR OF *THE QUICKENING MAZE*

Description is a violent act. A painting, said Picasso, is 'a horde of destructions'. Through description, reality is broken down and reassembled according to what you, the author, desire, what you want to see and feel. The resulting words must be formally satisfying, finding an artistic pattern that has only tangentially to do with lived experience per se and yet somehow renders it with the greatest possible intensity.

Description in fiction should always be at least as vivid as lived experience, generally more so. We make and drink a cup of tea without really thinking much about it. It happens in a kind of half-light of inattention, with things as they are taken for granted. But how much more brightly, gorgeously real it is when the cup isn't even in front of us and the milk instead is added by James Joyce in *Ulysses*: 'The sluggish cream wound curdling spirals through her tea.' Or later with this close-up on a *mélange* coffee (a kind of Viennese cappuccino) and a scone: 'He sank two lumps of sugar deftly longwise through the whipped cream. Buck Mulligan slit a steaming scone in two and plastered butter over its smoking pith.'

Both descriptions are made real by their spatial

precision ('spirals', 'longwise'), by their sensory alertness ('sluggish cream', 'smoking pith'), and by their music, attuned to the activities described. There are the long thick vowels of 'sluggish cream wound curdling spirals', which contrast with the lightly sprung, quick vowels and vivid labial consonants of 'Buck Mulligan slit a steaming scone in two and plastered butter over its smoking pith.' Sound, sense, space – everything arrives at once and the reader is engrossed with the particularity of the experience.

Description masters reality but it can only come after submission to experience, immersion in it. In *Four Quartets*, TS Eliot meditates on the difficulty of writing and refers to 'what there is to conquer/By strength or submission'. There is a subtle insight in the second of these possibilities. Not conquest or submission but conquest by submission. Joyce owns the wealth of experience – that slow spiral of cream, the smoking scone – through his submission to it, his open, rapt absorption. To write good description, therefore, you have to love the world, to gaze at it as at a lover's face, forgetful of yourself, immersed.

Description is, so to speak, a violent act, not only because it remakes the world but also because it dissolves and remakes the self. It is a kind of meditation, one that can procure bliss. Here is Flaubert reliving that liberation from the ordinary boundaries of being an individual person in a letter he wrote at two in the morning, after a day's work:

> No matter whether good or bad, it is a delectable
> thing, writing! not having to be yourself, being
> able to circulate in amongst the whole creation
> that you are describing. Today for instance, as
> a man and as a woman, as lover and mistress
> both, I have been out riding in a forest on an
> autumn afternoon, and I was the horses, the
> leaves, the wind, the words that they spoke to
> each other and the red sunlight that made them
> half-close their eyes, eyes that were brimming
> with love.

Notice how everything Flaubert talks about describing
plays an active part in the scene: the light, the horses,
the couple and their expressions. Nothing here is gratu-
itous and ornamental, everything is live and connected.
This is important. When literary writing declines
into fine writing it is often because description isn't
purposeful; rather, it's filler, virtuoso, it's pretty and in
supposed good taste.

We can see how careful Evelyn Waugh is to avoid
such a slackening in this deft paragraph from his
1934 novel *A Handful of Dust*. The paragraph is scene
setting, pure description, the creation of a landscape
in which events will unfold and that contrasts with
the environment in which the 'hero', Tony Last, will
end up:

> Outside, it was soft English weather; mist in the
> hollows and pale sunshine on the hills; the coverts
> had ceased dripping, for there were no leaves to
> hold the recent rain, but the undergrowth was
> wet, dark in the shadows, iridescent where the
> sun caught it; the lanes were soggy and there was
> water running in the ditches.

Waugh avoids indulgence by not spending too long on this description. The landscape is conjured with rapid notations that follow each other in a single sentence. Waugh resists the temptation to rhapsodise. There is a definite throb of patriotic feeling for this place in that phrase 'soft English weather' but what follows is not at all kitsch or sentimental. Certainly there is a note of rapture in that pale sunshine and iridescent undergrowth but it is earthed by the counterweight of dark shadows, leafless coverts, soggy lanes and gurgling ditches. None of the adjectives Waugh uses (with the single exception of 'iridescent') are high-sounding or unusual; they are commonplace and informal: soft, wet, dark, pale, soggy.

And this is all subtly to the point, contributing to the novel's story. The reader here learns how Tony Last's tenderness for this place is born of intimate knowledge. His relationship with it is a marriage, not an infatuation, and that makes his ultimate separation from it all the more painful. All this from Waugh's single sentence of description.

The current of story tends to flow more naturally through descriptions of action. Let's end with a
moment from Hemingway's short story 'The Capital
of the World'. Note how strictly Hemingway keeps to
the first-person perspective, how sharply attuned his
senses are as adrenaline flows through the character,
how he notices only what's important to the character, in close-up, how precisely Hemingway renders
the spatial arrangement of the matador's posture as
he strikes, how he makes the unfamiliar familiar with
a homely simile, how rapid action can be conveyed
indirectly by the confusing gaps in events after the
irrevocable has already happened. This is description at
its most purposeful and it quickens the pulse:

He could remember when he was good and it had
been only three years before. He could remember
the weight of his heavy gold-brocaded fighting
jacket on his shoulders on that hot afternoon in
May when his voice had still been the same in the
ring as in the cafe, and how he sighted along the
point-dipping blade at the place in the top of the
shoulders where it was dusty in the short-haired
black hump of muscle above the wide, wood-
knocking, splintered-tipped horns that lowered
as he went in to kill, and how the sword pushed
in as easy as into a mound of stiff butter with the
palm of his hand pushing the pommel, his left

arm crossed low, his left shoulder forward, his weight on his left leg, and then his weight wasn't on his leg. His weight was on his lower belly and as the bull raised his head the horn was out of sight in him and he swung over on it twice before they pulled him off it.

THE IMPORTANCE OF PLOT

KATE MOSSE, AUTHOR OF *LABYRINTH*

A story is just the stuff that happened; plot is the intrigue of how and why. Yet in writing courses and workbooks, plot is often the poor relation of those apparently superior skills of characterisation, dialogue and style.

Sometimes plot dare not speak its own name, going incognito as 'structure' or 'planning'. Stephen King, in *On Writing*, calls it 'the good writer's last resort and the dullard's first choice'. Ouch! For him, plotting is incompatible with the spontaneity of creation.

Yet a good plot is exactly what draws me to a novel in the first place. And keeps me there. Without it, no amount of sizzling dialogue or exquisite description or beautiful language is enough.

IT WASN'T ALWAYS LIKE THIS

What are the oldest stories we know of? Aboriginal Dreamtime tales are rich in incident – the characters do things and their actions cause change. Greek myths are full of challenges faced and met by interchangeable heroes. In his *Poetics*, Aristotle himself refers to plot as the most important element of drama, trumping character or setting or even language. The fourth-century BC polymath coined the truism 'beginning, middle and end' and recommended that the events should interconnect.

Fast forward to 1863. Gustav Freytag developed Aristotle's three parts into five: exposition, rising action, turning point, falling action and resolution. The exposition introduces the main characters – who they are and what they want. The plot is about how they try to get it. In screenwriting, we talk about the status quo, inciting events, through lines and crescendos. It's no coincidence that the story told in the sonata form I studied as a junior violinist goes like this: exposition, transition, development, recapitulation, coda.

WRITING WITH PURPOSE

A couple of weeks ago, taking refuge from the rain in a secondhand bookshop, I came upon a yellowed hardback published by Bodley Head in 1933. It was bound in brown ribbed board with the title, in red italics: *The Technique of Novel Writing: A Practical Guide for New Authors*. The author, Basil Hogarth, laments that: 'A tradition has been allowed to arise . . . more by default than by deliberate intention, that the novel possesses no technique; that its craft inherits no secrets . . . that, in the phrase of Henry James, it is a "sprawling invertebrate", a freak of literary creation.'

For me, a novel without a unifying plot is oddly without purpose – its individual stories lying adjacent but unresolved on the page. I sometimes wonder if the prejudice against plot is merely a new way to frame the conflict between literary and commercial. It's nothing new. Swift v Defoe, Dickens v Thackeray. There are, of course, wonderfully picaresque or dazzling episodic novels that revel in their lack of plot. But most authors are not Cervantes or Laurence Sterne.

PLAUSIBILITY

Aristotle advised that the story should convince. Characters must do and say the things that, if you met them, they would do and say. In Terence Rattigan's 1952 play *The Deep Blue Sea*, Hester Collyer leaves her husband, an eminent judge, for a flaky former RAF pilot who will never love her with the intensity with which she loves him. She attempts suicide, fails and conceals the attempt. But, because she loves him, she has written her lover a note to tell him not to blame himself. He finds the note and is tortured by the realisation that he drove her so far

This is the device – and on stage the scrutiny is intense. Does it convince? Without the stumbled-upon letter there will be no chain of interconnected events, driving the action forward to the final, redemptive scene.

It's this tricksy little word, 'device'. Perhaps there have been too many letters pushed under doormats and never found, cars that don't start, mobiles out of battery – what again? – and conversations coincidentally overheard. These are the dull tricks Stephen King rightly condemns. In the hands of Rattigan, though, every event has earned its place.

THE PROMISE

Plots may be visible. In Dan Brown's *The Lost Symbol* we collect new facts like Brownies collect badges and every piece of information – how it is given, when it is given – has some bearing on the story.

Plots may be subtly concealed. In Agatha Christie's *Five Little Pigs*, Carla Lemarchant is engaged to be married but dares not proceed. Her mother was convicted of the murder of her husband, Amyas Crale, 16 years earlier. Poirot investigates. We learn everything that he learns, down to the central, incontrovertible clue – the words pronounced by Amyas shortly before he died – and we wonder. Of course we know that Poirot knows and that, in the end, Agatha Christie will keep her promise – the plot that underlies the story will be revealed.

I know very quickly whether or not I will enjoy a novel. There's an attractive conviction to the writing of authors that I trust – I know they won't waste my time. In the end, everything counts.

THE SPACES BETWEEN

I'm not advocating suffocating novels, plotted into submission. Good novels are completed by their readers. Bad novels are completed by their authors: overwritten, over-detailed and over-plotted.

But plot needn't be a straitjacket, rather a sturdy skeleton over which the beautiful drapery of dialogue, characterisation, period and location can be shown off to best advantage. Then, if you are at all like me, when you get to the end and all has finally become clear, you can say to yourself: 'Of course!' Because that's what plot is – the hidden chain of cause and effect that it takes a whole novel to explain.

CREATING SUSPENSE

MARK BILLINGHAM, AUTHOR OF *SLEEPYHEAD*

I am often asked how you go about creating suspense. There was a period when, in answer to this question, I would talk about the tricks of the trade: the cliffhanger, the twist and the 'reveal'. Such things are still important, but I have come to realise that the answer actually lies in something far more basic, something that should be central to the writing of any piece of fiction: the creation of character.

The techniques mentioned above are, of course, all vital pieces of the mystery writer's armoury and, as such, are components of the genre that readers of crime novels have come to expect. They are part of the package; the buttons that a writer has to push every so often. When a crime writer thinks up a delicious twist, it is a great moment. Time to relax and take the rest of the day off. I do think that it can be overdone, however. There are a number of writers who believe it is their duty to throw as many curve balls at the reader as possible. To twist and twist again. These are the Chubby Checkers of crime fiction and, while I admire the craft, I think that it can actually work against genuine suspense. Put simply, I find it hard to engage with any book that is no more than a demonstration of technique.

That said, the 'reveal' remains a very effective technique, and one with which I am very familiar from my time as a standup comedian. It may sound surprising, but a joke and a crime novel work in very much the same way. The comedian/writer leads their audience along the garden path. The audience know what's coming, or at least they think they do until they get hit from a direction they were not expecting.

The best example I can think of from the world of crime fiction is in Thomas Harris's novel, *The Silence of the Lambs*. The Swat team have the killer cornered and are approaching his house. At the same time, Clarice Starling has been dispatched to a small town many miles away to tie up a few loose ends. A member of the Swat team rings the killer's doorbell. We cut to the killer's ghastly cellar where he hears the doorbell ring. This is the moment when the dummy is sold and the reader buys it completely. The reader stays with the killer as he slowly climbs the stairs. We know he has a gun. We know what he is capable of. He opens the door, and. . . it's Clarice Starling! The Swat team are at the wrong house, she is at the right house and she doesn't know it. It's the perfect reveal and it happens at the precise moment that the reader turns the page. The best crime fiction is full of heart-stopping moments such as this.

The reason that Harris's reveal works so wonderfully, however, is not just the sublime timing. It works because of the character of Clarice Starling, a young woman the reader has come to know well and to empathise with. Ultimately, this is where I believe that the key to genuine suspense is to be found.

This revelation happened several years ago when I was reading a novel called *The Turnaround* by American writer George Pelecanos. Pelecanos is happy enough to call himself a crime writer, but he is not one overly concerned with the sort of tricks already described. There is usually shocking violence, often with an element of investigation in its aftermath, but his books are not traditional mysteries by any means. What he does do is create characters that live and breathe on the page. As I read, I realised I had come to know some of these people so well that the idea that something bad was going to happen to them had become almost unbearable. I was turning each page with a sense of dread and it dawned on me that here was the most satisfying way to create suspense.

These are crime novels, after all. The reader has seen the jacket, read the blurb and knows very well what they are in for. Yes, there may be redemption and resolution of a sort, but there will also be suffering and pain, grief and dreadful loss. You know it's coming, but not when or to whom. The tension is real and terrible, because you care.

So, by all means throw in a thrilling twist every now and again, but not so often that they lose their power to shock. Time those 'reveals' to perfection so as to give your reader a punch line they will remember for a long time. But above all, give your readers characters they genuinely care about, that have the power to move them, and you will have suspense from page one.

REVISING AND REWRITING

MJ HYLAND, AUTHOR OF *CARRY ME DOWN*

I've never read or written a perfect first draft. Perfect first drafts don't exist. And yet most writers, at the beginning of their careers, think they must. This intimidating myth of effortless gift persists because successful authors aren't in the habit of admitting to writing weak drafts and rarely show the public their mistakes.

> *'Every writer I know has trouble writing'*
> – Joseph Heller

The truth is that every beautiful, exciting and moving work of fiction is last in a line of at least a half-dozen carefully reworked drafts. Good writers are good because they have the right measure of intellect and talent for the hard labour of rewriting. Most writers haven't the stamina for this exacting work, or are too thin-skinned, defensive or impatient to face the bad news that they haven't got it right the first time round.

Rewriting accounts for the lion's share of a writer's work; the calculated and deliberate work that comes after the gleeful, and sometimes unconscious, first draft. Good writers, even the arrogant ones, are also humble and self-aware enough to know that revision is always necessary.

FIXING THE FIRST DRAFT

'If it sounds like writing, I rewrite it'
– Elmore Leonard

Here are seven techniques that are sure to make your job of revision easier and more effective:

1   Remove exaggeration (tell the fictional 'truth'). *'The great enemy of clear language is insincerity. When there is a gap between one's real and one's declared aims, one turns instinctively to long words and exhausted idioms, like a cuttlefish squirting out ink'* – George Orwell

2   Cut out clichés. *'Don't tell me the moon is shining; show me the glint of light on broken glass'* – Anton Chekhov

3   Remove your failed similes. A bad simile is embarrassing, like a long joke with a weak punch line, told by a nervous comedian. *'Kate inched over her own thoughts like a measuring worm'* – John Steinbeck

4   Don't attempt a final version of the beginning of the story until you know how it ends. (And don't waste time fussing over the beginning until the rest of the work is done.) *'Be direct, simple, brief, vigorous and lucid'* – HW Fowler

5   Do at least one of the following to help you see your prose more clearly:

- Write by hand
- Use an ugly font
- Read your work aloud, or have somebody else read it aloud
- Write your second draft without referring to the first draft

'Have something to say, and say it as clearly as you can. That is the only secret of style'
– Matthew Arnold

6   Don't use more words than you need to and beware of fancy or ornate words. *'I never write "metropolis" for seven cents when I can write "city" and get paid the same'* – Mark Twain

7   Make sure your adverbs and adjectives aren't muting your verbs and nouns. *'The road to hell is paved with adverbs'* – Stephen King

AN EXAMPLE OF POOR PROSE

This is typical of the kind of thing I see in early drafts every day, and it can be cured, in time, if the writer has the right kind of talent and intelligence, and by applying the above principles:

The smell in the crowded pub was so vile that I nearly gagged. It was like the smell of a camel that's been dead for three days. I whispered under my breath to Sarah, 'That smell is so disgusting,' and Sarah nodded so violently I thought her head would fall off, but she still looked beautiful with all her red curls wrapping round themselves like the golden tendrils of an ancient oak tree or like the snakes on Medusa's head that we saw in the museum last week.

This bad prose is very bad. The descriptions are overwrought, dilute dramatic effect and undermine authorial and narrative credibility. To say 'nearly gagged' is not just clichéd, it's barely credible. Something prosaic is better than the wrecking-ball of 'gagged'. A more subtle and truer description of the smell would better serve to establish trust between reader and writer. Something like, 'The pub smelt of whisky and vegetable soup.' Most people know what whisky and vegetable soup smell like, but few know the smell of 'a camel that's been dead for three days'. And the 'crowded pub' is probably noisy, so the idea of 'whispered under my breath' is tautological and untruthful.

As for the other errors, see if you can find them yourself and rewrite the paragraph knowing this: it's crucial that the reader not only sees what you want them to see but also believes you.

'The best style is the style you don't notice'
– Somerset Maugham

CURING THE FEAR OF INADEQUACY

Many fledgling writers suffer from a problem that turns their prose into overblown mush: the idea that good writing is fancy writing, packed with complicated writerly flourish, staggering similes and metaphors, and that all great writing begins with a knock-out opening sentence.

Through most of my early 20s I thought the same. There was panic and lots of wasted, misdirected effort – time spent glued to the idea that I must prove my intelligence, at the cost of worrying about much more important things, such as character and truthful storytelling. I gave up chasing similes as good as Nabokov's, and thought more about Chekhov's compassion for character, and the brutal and compelling grace of Flannery O'Connor's fiction. I stopped showing off and set out to write drama void of conspicuous artifice.

When I quit trying to sound like a writer, I became more of a writer. I took my desire to impress off the page and listened to Leo Tolstoy:

> Drama, instead of telling us the whole of a man's life, must place him in such a situation, tie such a knot, that when it is untied, the whole man is visible.

MY
RULES

DOS AND DON'TS FROM THE GREATS

DIANA ATHILL

1 Read it aloud to yourself because that's the only way to be sure the rhythms of the sentences are OK (prose rhythms are too complex and subtle to be thought out – they can be got right only by ear).

2 Cut (perhaps that should be CUT): only by having *no* inessential words can every essential word be made to count.

3 You don't always have to go so far as to murder your darlings – those turns of phrase or images of which you felt extra-proud when they appeared on the page – but go back and look at them with *a very beady eye*. Almost always it turns out that they'd be better dead. (Not every little twinge of satisfaction is suspect – it's the ones that amount to a sort of smug glee you must watch out for.)

1   Take a pencil to write with on aeroplanes. Pens leak. But if the pencil breaks, you can't sharpen it on the plane, because you can't take knives with you. Therefore: take two pencils.

2   If both pencils break, you can do a rough sharpening job with a nail file of the metal or glass type.

3   Take something to write on. Paper is good. In a pinch, pieces of wood or your arm will do.

4   If you're using a computer, always safeguard new text with a memory stick.

5   Do back exercises. Pain is distracting.

6   Hold the reader's attention. (This is likely to work better if you can hold your own.) But you don't know who the reader is, so it's like shooting fish with a slingshot in the dark. What fascinates A will bore the pants off B.

7   You most likely need a thesaurus, a rudimentary grammar book, and a grip on reality. This latter means: there's no free lunch. Writing is work. It's also gambling. You don't get a pension plan. Other people can help you a bit, but essentially you're on your own. Nobody is making you do this: you chose it, so don't whine.

8   You can never read your own book with the innocent anticipation that comes with that first delicious

.page of a new book, because you wrote the thing. You've been backstage. You've seen how the rabbits were smuggled into the hat. Therefore ask a reading friend or two to look at it before you give it to anyone in the publishing business. This friend should not be someone with whom you have a romantic relationship, unless you want to break up.

9 Don't sit down in the middle of the woods. If you're lost in the plot or blocked, retrace your steps to where you went wrong. Then take the other road. And/or change the person. Change the tense. Change the opening page.

10 Prayer might work. Or reading something else. Or a constant visualisation of the holy grail that is the finished, published version of your resplendent book.

1   Do not place a photograph of your favourite author on your desk, especially if the author is one of the famous ones who committed suicide.

2   Do be kind to yourself. Fill pages as quickly as possible; double space, or write on every second line. Regard every new page as a small triumph. . .

3   Until you get to page 50. Then calm down, and start worrying about the quality. Do feel anxiety – it's the job.

4   Do give the work a name as quickly as possible. Own it, and see it. Dickens knew *Bleak House* was going to be called *Bleak House* before he started writing it. The rest must have been easy.

5   Do restrict your browsing to a few websites a day. Don't go near the online bookies – unless it's research.

6   Do keep a thesaurus, but in the shed at the back of the garden or behind the fridge, somewhere that demands travel or effort. Chances are the words that come into your head will do fine, e.g. 'horse', 'ran', 'said'.

7   Do, occasionally, give in to temptation. Wash the kitchen floor, hang out the washing. It's research.

8   Do change your mind. Good ideas are often murdered by better ones. I was working on a novel

about a band called the Partitions. Then I decided to call them the Commitments.

9   Do not search amazon.co.uk for the book you haven't written yet.

10 Do spend a few minutes a day working on the cover biog – 'He divides his time between Kabul and Tierra del Fuego.' But then get back to work.

HELEN DUNMORE

1 Finish the day's writing when you still want to continue.

2 Listen to what you have written. A dud rhythm in a passage of dialogue may show that you don't yet understand the characters well enough to write in their voices.

3 Read Keats's letters.

4 Reread, rewrite, reread, rewrite. If it still doesn't work, throw it away. It's a nice feeling, and you don't want to be cluttered with the corpses of poems and stories that have everything in them except the life they need.

5 Learn poems by heart.

6 Join professional organisations that advance the collective rights of authors.

7 A problem with a piece of writing often clarifies itself if you go for a long walk.

8 If you fear that taking care of your children and household will damage your writing, think of JG Ballard.

9 Don't worry about posterity – as Larkin (no sentimentalist) observed, 'What will survive of us is love.'

... ✐

GEOFF DYER

1 Never worry about the commercial possibilities of a project. That stuff is for agents and editors to fret over – or not. Conversation with my American publisher. Me: 'I'm writing a book so boring, of such limited commercial appeal, that if you publish it, it will probably cost you your job.' Publisher: 'That's exactly what makes me want to stay in my job.'

2 Don't write in public places. In the early 1990s I went to live in Paris. The usual writerly reasons: back then, if you were caught writing in a pub in England, you could get your head kicked in, whereas in Paris, *dans les cafés*. . . Since then I've developed an aversion to writing in public. I now think it should be done only in private, like any other lavatorial activity.

3 Don't be one of those writers who sentence themselves to a lifetime of sucking up to Nabokov.

4 If you use a computer, constantly refine and expand your autocorrect settings. The only reason I stay loyal to my piece-of-shit computer is that I have invested so much ingenuity into building one of the great autocorrect files in literary history. Perfectly formed and spelt words emerge from a few brief keystrokes: 'Niet' becomes 'Nietzsche', 'phoy' becomes 'photography' and so on. Genius!

5 Keep a diary. The biggest regret of my writing life is that I have never kept a journal or a diary.

6 Have regrets. They are fuel. On the page they flare into desire.

7 Have more than one idea on the go at any one time. If it's a choice between writing a book and doing nothing I will always choose the latter. It's only if I have an idea for two books that I choose one rather than the other. I always have to feel that I'm bunking off from *something*.

8 Beware of clichés. Not just the clichés that Martin Amis is at war with. There are clichés of response as well as expression. There are clichés of observation and of thought – even of conception. Many novels, even quite a few adequately written ones, are clichés of *form* that conform to clichés of expectation.

9 Do it every day. Make a habit of putting your observations into words and gradually this will become instinct. This is the most important rule of all and, naturally, I don't follow it.

10 Never ride a bike with the brakes on. If something is proving too difficult, give up and do something else. Try to live without resort to perseverance. But writing is all about perseverance. You've got to stick at it. In my 30s I used to go to the gym even though I hated it. The purpose of going to the gym was to postpone the day when I would stop going. That's what writing is to me: a way of postponing the day

when I won't do it any more, the day when I will
sink into a depression so profound it will be indis-
tinguishable from perfect bliss.

ANNE ENRIGHT

1   The first 12 years are the worst.

2   The way to write a book is to actually *write* a book. A pen is useful, typing is also good. Keep putting words on the page.

3   Only bad writers think that their work is really good.

4   Description is hard. Remember that all description is an opinion about the world. Find a place to stand.

5   Write whatever way you like. Fiction is made of words on a page; reality is made of something else. It doesn't matter how 'real' your story is, or how 'made up': what matters is its necessity.

6   Try to be accurate about stuff.

7   Imagine that you are dying. If you had a terminal disease would you finish this book? Why not? The thing that annoys this 10-weeks-to-live self is the thing that is wrong with the book. So change it. Stop arguing with yourself. Change it. See? Easy. And no one had to die.

8   You can also do all that with whiskey.

9   Have fun.

10 Remember, if you sit at your desk for 15 or 20 years, every day, not counting weekends, it changes you. It just does. It may not improve your temper, but it fixes something else. It makes you more free.

RICHARD FORD

1   Marry somebody you love and who thinks you being a writer's a good idea.
2   Don't have children.
3   Don't read your reviews.
4   Don't write reviews. (Your judgment's always tainted.)
5   Don't have arguments with your wife in the morning, or late at night.
6   Don't drink and write at the same time.
7   Don't write letters to the editor. (No one cares.)
8   Don't wish ill on your colleagues.
9   Try to think of others' good luck as encouragement to yourself.
10   Don't take any shit if you can possibly help it.

...✎

ESTHER FREUD

1   When in doubt cut out the metaphors and similes. In my first book I promised myself I wouldn't use any and I slipped up during a sunset in chapter 11. I still blush when I come across it.

2   A story needs rhythm. Read it aloud to yourself. If it doesn't spin a bit of magic, it's missing something.

3   Editing is everything. Cut until you can cut no more. What is left often springs into life.

4   Find your best time of the day for writing and write. Don't let anything else interfere. Afterwards it won't matter to you that the kitchen is a mess.

5   Don't wait for inspiration. Discipline is the key.

6   Trust your reader. Not everything needs to be explained. If you really know something, and breathe life into it, they'll know it too.

7   Never forget: even your own rules are there to be broken.

NEIL GAIMAN

1 Write.

2 Put one word after another. Find the right word, put it down.

3 Finish what you're writing. Whatever you have to do to finish it, finish it.

4 Put it aside. Read it pretending you've never read it before. Show it to friends whose opinion you respect and who like the kind of thing that this is.

5 Remember: when people tell you something's wrong or doesn't work for them, they are almost always right. When they tell you exactly what they think is wrong and how to fix it, they are almost always wrong.

6 Fix it. Remember that, sooner or later, before it ever reaches perfection, you will have to let it go and move on and start to write the next thing. Perfection is like chasing the horizon. Keep moving.

7 Laugh at your own jokes.

8 The main rule of writing is that if you do it with enough assurance and confidence, you're allowed to do whatever you like. (That may be a rule for life as well as for writing. But it's definitely true for writing.) So write your story as it needs to be written. Write it honestly, and tell it as best you can. I'm not sure that there are any other rules. Not ones that matter.

...✒

DAVID HARE

1   Write only when you have something to say.
2   Never take advice from anyone with no investment in the outcome.
3   Style is the art of getting yourself out of the way, not putting yourself in it.
4   If nobody will put your play on, put it on yourself.
5   Jokes are like hands and feet for a painter. They may not be what you want to end up doing but you have to master them in the meanwhile.
6   Theatre primarily belongs to the young.
7   No one has ever achieved consistency as a screenwriter.
8   Never go to a TV personality festival masquerading as a literary festival.
9   Never complain of being misunderstood. You can choose to be understood, or you can choose not to.
10 The two most depressing words in the English language are 'literary fiction'.

PD JAMES

1. Increase your word power. Words are the raw material of our craft. The greater your vocabulary, the more effective your writing. We who write in English are fortunate to have the richest and most versatile language in the world. Respect it.

2. Read widely and with discrimination. Bad writing is contagious.

3. Don't just plan to write – write. It is only by writing, not dreaming about it, that we develop our own style.

4. Write what you need to write, not what is currently popular or what you think will sell.

5. Open your mind to new experiences, particularly to the study of other people. Nothing that happens to a writer – however happy, however tragic – is ever wasted.

...✎

AL KENNEDY

1   Have humility. Older/more experienced/more
    convincing writers may offer rules and varieties
    of advice. Consider what they say. However, don't
    automatically give them charge of your brain,
    or anything else – they might be bitter, twisted,
    burned-out, manipulative, or just not very like you.
2   Have more humility. Remember you don't know
    the limits of your own abilities. Successful or not,
    if you keep pushing beyond yourself, you will
    enrich your own life – and maybe even please a
    few strangers.
3   Defend others. You can, of course, steal stories and
    attributes from family and friends, fill in filecards
    after lovemaking and so forth. It might be better to
    celebrate those you love – and love itself – by writ-
    ing in such a way that everyone keeps their privacy
    and dignity intact.
4   Defend your work. Organisations, institutions and
    individuals will often think they know best about
    your work – especially if they are paying you.
    When you genuinely believe their decisions would
    damage your work – walk away. Run away. The
    money doesn't matter that much.
5   Defend yourself. Find out what keeps you happy,
    motivated and creative.

6 Write. No amount of self-inflicted misery, altered states, black pullovers or being publicly obnoxious will ever add up to your being a writer. Writers write. On you go.

7 Read. As much as you can. As deeply and widely and nourishingly and irritatingly as you can. And the good things will make you remember them, so you won't need to take notes.

8 Be without fear. This is impossible, but let the small fears drive your rewriting and set aside the large ones until they behave – then use them, maybe even write them. Too much fear and all you'll get is silence.

9 Remember you love writing. It wouldn't be worth it if you didn't. If the love fades, do what you need to and get it back.

10 Remember writing doesn't love you. It doesn't care. Nevertheless, it can behave with remarkable generosity. Speak well of it, encourage others, pass it on.

1   Are you serious about this? Then get an accountant.

2   Read *Becoming a Writer*, by Dorothea Brande. Then do what it says, including the tasks you think are impossible. You will particularly hate the advice to write first thing in the morning, but if you can manage it, it might well be the best thing you ever do for yourself. This book is about becoming a writer from the inside out. Many later advice manuals derive from it. You don't really need any others, though if you want to boost your confidence, 'how to' books seldom do any harm. You can kick-start a whole book with some little writing exercise.

3   Write a book you'd like to read. If you wouldn't read it, why would anybody else? Don't write for a perceived audience or market. It may well have vanished by the time your book's ready.

4   If you have a good story idea, don't assume it must form a prose narrative. It may work better as a play, a screenplay or a poem. Be flexible.

5   Be aware that anything that appears before 'chapter one' may be skipped. Don't put your vital clue there.

6   First paragraphs can often be struck out. Are you performing a haka, or just shuffling your feet?

7   Concentrate your narrative energy on the point of change. This is especially important for historical

fiction. When your character is new to a place, or things alter around them, that's the point to step back and fill in the details of their world. People don't notice their everyday surroundings and daily routine, so when writers describe them it can sound as if they're trying too hard to instruct the reader.

8   Description must work for its place. It can't be simply ornamental. It usually works best if it has a human element: it is more effective if it comes from an implied viewpoint, rather than from the eye of God. If description is coloured by the viewpoint of the character who is doing the noticing, it becomes, in effect, part of character definition and part of the action.

9   If you get stuck, get away from your desk. Take a walk, take a bath, go to sleep, make a pie, draw, listen to music, meditate, exercise: whatever you do, don't just stick there scowling at the problem. But don't make telephone calls or go to a party: if you do, other people's words will pour in where your lost words should be. Open a gap for them, create a space. Be patient.

10 Be ready for anything. Each new story has different demands and may throw up reasons to break these and all other rules. Except number one: you can't give your soul to literature if you're thinking about income tax.

...✒

MICHAEL MOORCOCK

1   My first rule was given to me by TH White, author of *The Sword in the Stone* and other Arthurian fantasies and was: read. Read everything you can lay hands on. I always advise people who want to write a fantasy or science fiction or romance to stop reading everything in those genres and start reading everything else from Bunyan to Byatt.

2   Find an author you admire (mine was Conrad) and copy their plots and characters in order to tell your own story, just as people learn to draw and paint by copying the masters.

3   Introduce your main characters and themes in the first third of your novel.

4   If you are writing a plot-driven genre novel make sure all your major themes/plot elements are introduced in the first third, which you can call the *introduction*.

5   Develop your themes and characters in your second third, the *development*.

6   Resolve your themes, mysteries and so on in the final third, the *resolution*.

7   For a good melodrama study the famous 'Lester Dent master plot formula' which you can find online. It was written to show how to write a short story for the pulps, but can be adapted successfully for most stories of any length or genre.

8   If possible have something going on while you have
    your characters delivering exposition or philoso-
    phising. This helps retain dramatic tension.

9   Carrot and stick – have protagonists pursued (by an
    obsession or a villain) and pursuing (idea, object,
    person, mystery).

10 Ignore all proffered rules and create your own,
    suitable for what you want to say.

ANDREW MOTION

1 Decide when in the day (or night) it best suits you to write, and organise your life accordingly.
2 Think with your senses as well as your brain.
3 Honour the miraculousness of the ordinary.
4 Lock different characters/elements in a room and tell them to get on.
5 Remember there is no such thing as nonsense.
6 Bear in mind Wilde's dictum that 'only mediocrities develop' – and challenge it.
7 Let your work stand before deciding whether or not to serve.
8 Think big and stay particular.
9 Write for tomorrow, not for today.
10 Work hard.

... ✐

JOYCE CAROL OATES

1   Don't try to anticipate an 'ideal reader' – there may be one, but he/she is reading someone else.

2   Don't try to anticipate an 'ideal reader' – except for yourself perhaps, sometime in the future.

3   Be your own editor/critic. Sympathetic but merciless!

4   Unless you are writing something very avant-garde – all gnarled, snarled and 'obscure' – be alert for possibilities of paragraphing.

5   Unless you are writing something very post-modernist – self-conscious, self-reflexive and 'provocative' – be alert for possibilities of using plain familiar words in place of polysyllabic 'big' words.

6   Keep in mind Oscar Wilde: 'A little sincerity is a dangerous thing, and a great deal of it is absolutely fatal.'

7   Keep a light, hopeful heart. But expect the worst.

ANNIE PROULX

1   Proceed slowly and take care.
2   To ensure that you proceed slowly, write by hand.
3   Write slowly and by hand only about subjects that interest you.
4   Develop craftsmanship through years of wide reading.
5   Rewrite and edit until you achieve the most felicitous phrase/sentence/paragraph/page/story/chapter.

IAN RANKIN

1 Read lots.
2 Write lots.
3 Learn to be self-critical.
4 Learn what criticism to accept.
5 Be persistent.
6 Have a story worth telling.
7 Don't give up.
8 Know the market.
9 Get lucky.
10 Stay lucky.

...✒

1   Don't look back until you've written an entire draft, just begin each day from the last sentence you wrote the preceeding day. This prevents those cringing feelings, and means that you have a substantial body of work before you get down to the real work which is all in. . .

2   The edit.

3   Always carry a notebook. And I mean *always*. The short-term memory only retains information for three minutes; unless it is committed to paper you can lose an idea for ever.

4   Stop reading fiction – it's all lies anyway, and it doesn't have anything to tell you that you don't know already (assuming, that is, you've read a great deal of fiction in the past; if you haven't you have no business whatsoever being a writer of fiction).

5   You know that sickening feeling of inadequacy and over-exposure you feel when you look upon your own empurpled prose? Relax into the awareness that this ghastly sensation will never, ever leave you, no matter how successful and publicly lauded you become. It is intrinsic to the real business of writing and should be cherished.

6   Live life and write about life. Of the making of

many books there is indeed no end, but there are more than enough books about books.

7   By the same token remember how much time people spend watching TV. If you're writing a novel with a contemporary setting there need to be long passages where nothing happens save for TV watching: 'Later, George watched *Grand Designs* while eating HobNobs. Later still he watched the shopping channel for a while. . .'

8   The writing life is essentially one of solitary confinement – if you can't deal with this you needn't apply.

9   Oh, and not forgetting the occasional beating administered by the sadistic guards of the imagination.

10 Regard yourself as a small corporation of one. Take yourself off on team-building exercises (long walks). Hold a Christmas party every year at which you stand in the corner of your writing room, shouting very loudly to yourself while drinking a bottle of white wine. Then masturbate under the desk. The following day you will feel a deep and cohering sense of embarrassment.

COLM TÓIBÍN

1. Finish everything you start.
2. Get on with it.
3. Stay in your mental pyjamas all day.
4. Stop feeling sorry for yourself.
5. No alcohol, sex or drugs while you are working.
6. Work in the morning, a short break for lunch, work in the afternoon and then watch the six o'clock news and then go back to work until bed-time. Before bed, listen to Schubert, preferably some songs.
7. If you have to read, to cheer yourself up read biographies of writers who went insane.
8. On Saturdays, you can watch an old Bergman film, preferably *Persona* or *Autumn Sonata*.
9. No going to London.
10. No going anywhere else either.

ROSE TREMAIN

1. Forget the boring old dictum, 'Write about what you know.' Instead, seek out an unknown yet knowable area of experience that's going to enhance your understanding of the world and write about that.

2. Nevertheless, remember that in the particularity of your own life lies the seed corn that will feed your imaginative work. So don't throw it all away on autobiography. (There are quite enough writers' memoirs out there already.)

3. Never be satisfied with a first draft. In fact, never be satisfied with your own stuff at all, until you're certain it's as good as your finite powers can enable it to be.

4. Listen to the criticisms and preferences of your trusted 'first readers'.

5. When an idea comes, spend silent time with it. Remember Keats's idea of Negative Capability and Kipling's advice to 'drift, wait and obey'. Along with your gathering of hard data, allow yourself also to dream your idea into being.

6. In the planning stage of a book, don't plan the ending. It has to be earned by all that will go before it.

7. Respect the way characters may change once they've got 50 pages of life in them. Revisit your plan at this stage and see whether certain things have to be altered to take account of these changes.

8   If you're writing historical fiction, don't have well-known real characters as your main protagonists. This will only create biographical unease in the readers and send them back to the history books. If you must write about real people, then do something postmodern and playful with them.

9   Learn from cinema. Be economic with descriptions. Sort out the telling detail from the lifeless one. Write dialogue that people would actually speak.

10 Never begin the book when you feel you want to begin it, but hold off a while longer.

JEANETTE WINTERSON

1 Turn up for work. Discipline allows creative freedom. No discipline equals no freedom.

2 Never stop when you are stuck. You may not be able to solve the problem, but turn aside and write something else. Do not stop altogether.

3 Love what you do.

4 Be honest with yourself. If you are no good, accept it. If the work you are doing is no good, accept it.

5 Don't hold on to poor work. If it was bad when it went in the drawer it will be just as bad when it comes out.

6 Take no notice of anyone you don't respect.

7 Take no notice of anyone with a gender agenda. A lot of men still think that women lack imagination of the fiery kind.

8 Be ambitious for the work and not for the reward.

9 Trust your creativity.

10 Enjoy this work!

...✒

HOW I WROTE...

WROTE...

THE MAKING OF MODERN CLASSICS

TIME'S ARROW

MARTIN AMIS

'Why did you decide to write a novel about the Holocaust?'
This challenge, which I still sometimes hear, can only be
answered as follows: 'But I never did.' Similarly, I never
decided to write a novel about teenage sexuality, or Thatcher's England, or millennial London, or, indeed, about the
Gulag (which I nonetheless completed in 2006). With
its hopelessly inapposite verb, and presumptuous prep-
osition, the question reveals an understandable naivety
about the way that fictions are made. For the novel, as
Norman Mailer put it, is 'the spooky art'.

Deciding to write a novel about something – as
opposed to finding you are writing a novel around
something – sounds to me like a good evocation of writer's block. No matter what its length (vignette, novella,
epic), a work of fiction begins with an inkling: a notion
that is also a physical sensation. It is hard to improve
on Nabokov, who variously described it as a 'shiver' and
a 'throb'. The throb can come from anywhere, a newspaper report (very common), the remnants of a dream,
a half-remembered quote. The crucial, the enabling
fermentation lies in this: the shiver must connect to
something already present in the subconscious.

Time's Arrow depended on a coincidence, or a
confluence. In the mid-1980s I started spending the

summers in Cape Cod, Massachusetts, where I made
friends with the distinguished 'psychohistorian' Robert
Jay Lifton. Bob was and is the author of a succession
of books on the political horrors of the 20th century:
books on thought reform in China, on Hiroshima, on
Vietnam. And in 1987 he gave me a copy of his latest
(and perhaps most celebrated) work, *The Nazi Doctors:
Medical Killing and the Psychology of Genocide*.

Here, Lifton's historiographical mission is to establish Nazism as an essentially biomedical ideology. It is
there in *Mein Kampf*: 'Anyone who wants to cure this
era, which is inwardly sick and rotten, must first of all
summon up the courage to make clear the causes of
this disease.' The Jew was the agent of 'racial pollu-
tion' and 'racial tuberculosis': the 'eternal bloodsucker',
'germ-carrier', the 'maggot in a rotting corpse'. Accordingly, the doctor must become a 'biological soldier';
the healer must become a killer. In the camps, all the
non-random murders were supervised by doctors (and
so were the crematoria). As one of their number put
it: 'Out of respect for human life, I would remove a
gangrenous appendix from a diseased body. The Jew
is the gangrenous appendix in the body of mankind.'

That year, too, I already had it in my head that I
might attempt a short story about a life lived backwards
in time. This tenuous proposition appealed to me as a
poetic possibility – but it seemed fatally frictionless. I
could find no application for a life so lived. Which life?
As I began *The Nazi Doctors*, I found myself thinking,

most disconcertingly, *this* life. The life of a Nazi doctor. 'Born' in New England, as an old man; 'dying' in Austria, in the 1920s, as a baby boy. . .

After more than a year of further reading, and of daily struggles with a sense of profanity and panic (by what entitlement could I address this sepulchral subject, and from such an apparently 'playful' vantage?), I began to write. And at once I made an emboldening discovery: the arrow of time turns out to be the arrow of reason or logic, expectably enough; but it is also the arrow of morality. Set the cinema of life in reverse motion, and (for example) Hiroshima is created in a single moment; violence is benign; killing becomes healing, healing kill-ing; the hospital is a torture chamber, the death camp a fount of life. Reverse the arrow of time, and the Nazi project becomes what Hitler said it was: the means to make Germany whole. Which still strikes me as some kind of measure of this terminal and diametrical atroc-ity: it asked for the arrow of time to point the other way.

We often ask ourselves who was worse: the little moustache or the big moustache, Hitler or Stalin? Well, 15 years later I wrote a novel about the Russian holocaust, too (*House of Meetings*); and the latter, inci-dentally, was the more difficult to write, because it focused on the victims and not the perpetrators. But that is by the way. In our hierarchy of evil, we instinc-tively promote Hitler. And we are right.

The Gulag – and this is not widely grasped – was first and foremost a system of state slavery. The goal, never achieved, was to make money. Still, this is a motive we can recognise. The German idea, with its 'dreams of omnipotence and sadism' (Lifton), was utterly inhuman, or 'counter-human', in Primo Levi's judgment, like a counter-clock world. The Nazis were on the intellectual level of the supermarket tabloid. It should not surprise us to learn that there was a government department, in Berlin, set up to prove that the Aryans were not descended from the apes; no, they came from the lost continent of Atlantis, in the heavens, where they were preserved in ice from the beginning of time.

THE SECRET DIARY OF
ADRIAN MOLE, AGED 13¾

SUE TOWNSEND

I had one ambition when I was a child, and that was to grow up and become an adult. I couldn't wait to get the hell out of childhood.

I was a secretive, reckless girl, who enjoyed sitting on the swaying top branch of a tree, looking down on the everyday world. Acute curiosity led me to explore the Leicestershire countryside. I set off on my Pink Witch bike. I didn't have a companion. Companions were forever whining that they were tired and hungry and wanted the toilet. When I got hungry I would search for a specific grass. It had velvety leaves and a sweet inner stalk. While I nibbled on the stalk I read my book. There was always a book – I knew no child who read with the same passion as me. After visiting the village church and listening to the loudness of the silence and saying hello to Jesus, I would pedal home in the twilight. Nobody asked me where I'd been, and I didn't volunteer the information.

I left school at 14. I was an Easter leaver, a no-hoper. But since being taught about infinity I felt that nothing really mattered, that we humans were transient specks in the universe. I had started to arrive late at school, I stopped doing my homework, I played truant.

When teachers got angry I would switch off and think about infinity. Like many writers I had an influential English teacher – pale, austere Miss Morris, who expected us to learn a poem by heart each week: Shakespeare, Milton, GK Chesterton, Keats, Shelley, Sitwell, Wilde. . . We also wrote a weekly composition: 'A Day in the Life of a Penny' and 'I am a Chippendale Chair'. I lost a school writing competition because, as Miss Morris told me sadly, 'You used a cliché, Susan. Clouds like cotton wool.'

When I left school I continued to write, and because I knew it was no good, I kept my writing a secret – for 20 years. During this time I married, had three children, was deserted, had TB and was rehoused to a council estate. On one of those stultifying, dull Sunday afternoons, my eldest child asked: 'Mum, why don't we go to safari parks, like other families do?' This mild rebuke set off a memory of my adolescent self and my interior monologue, which was full of self-pity and harsh criticism of most institutions.

I heard the voice of Nigel Mole (later to become Adrian), and because he was such a conventional boy he had to have irresponsible parents, a respectable, fearless grandmother and an anarchic dog. I wrote about three months' worth of Mole's *Secret Diary* and put it away in a large cardboard box that the fridge came in. It joined 20 years' worth of bad poetry, unfinished short stories and song lyrics, mostly written in the small hours when the children were asleep.

I had three part-time jobs. During school hours I was a community worker, working with elderly people who'd been moved into tower blocks, leaving their dogs, cats, rabbits and neighbours behind. In the early evening I was a youth worker, working mostly with adolescent boys. At 9pm I caught a bus into town and went to my third job: waitress and barmaid at the Fish and Quart.

I was exhausted and lonely. Then I met my second husband and he encouraged me to join a writers' group at the Phoenix Theatre in Leicester. Within a year I had won a Thames Television playwright award (championed by John Mortimer) and I became resident writer at the Phoenix, which had a company of actors, one of whom was Nigel Bennett, who said he was auditioning for *Huckleberry Finn* and did I have anything suitable? That night I rummaged through my fridge box and found *The Secret Diary*.

The next day I handed Nigel Bennett the messy, handwritten pages. He typed them up. He didn't get the part, but he sent the pages to John Tydeman at BBC Drama. *The Secret Diary* was first broadcast on 2 January 1982 – John had sent the pages to Geoffrey Strachan at Methuen, the leading publisher of comedy and drama. Geoffrey asked for a synopsis for a book. I didn't know how to write a synopsis, so I sent him Adrian Mole's school report, and on the strength of that Geoffrey commissioned a book.

When I heard that Methuen were planning to publish 5,000 in hardback I rang Geoffrey and asked him not to print so many. 'It won't sell,' I told him. He said: 'I think it will.' He was right. It has sold more than 5 million copies worldwide, it's translated into 45 languages and is still in print after 28 years.

...✎

THE WOMAN IN BLACK

SUSAN HILL

When I am emailed by pupils studying *The Woman in Black* for GCSE and A-level, many refer to it as 'gothic', and indeed it forms part of a university course in gothic literature. But although the book has something in common with the pure gothic fiction of the 18th and 19th centuries, it is really only a distant cousin of the genre. It is a ghost story – not a horror story, not a thriller – and not a gothic novel; although the terms are often used very loosely, they are not by any means the same thing.

I set out to write a ghost story in the classic 19th-century tradition, a full-length one. There have never been many, writers perhaps having felt the form would not stretch successfully. By the time I began mine, in the 1980s, full-length ghost stories seemed to have died out altogether. I read and studied the Jameses, Henry and MR, and Dickens, and I also had beside me the 'bible' – *Night Visitors* by Julia Briggs (still the best study of the form).

The list of ingredients included atmosphere, a ghost, a haunted house and other places, and weather. A footnote to 'ghost' was a) of a human being; and b) with a purpose. There are dozens of little books of 'true' ghost stories, usually sorted by geographical location, but almost without exception the ghosts have no purpose and so the stories are ultimately unsatisfying. A headless horseman rides by, a phantom coach clatters down a dark road, a veiled lady drifts up a staircase and through a wall, a pale and misty child's face is glimpsed at a window – and that is all. The ghosts are there and they apparently go through the same motions again and again. It is ultimately uninteresting. There has to be more to fiction than that. There also has to be more than an easy manipulation of the reader's superficial emotions – unless making someone jump out of their skin is the writer's only aim. Not that trying to induce a delicious thrill of fear is bad – it is another form of entertainment, and what is wrong with being an entertainer? Dickens certainly considered himself to be one.

I knew my ghost story, like all my fiction, had to have a serious point and it was this that must sustain the length and underpin the sense of place, the creation of atmosphere and the events. But moral points come out of character, and I kept asking myself the question: 'Why does a ghost return to this life?' Perhaps to give information that they have withheld in life – the whereabouts of a will, say, or the identity of a murderer, or to warn. But my ghost returns to exact revenge and it is the nature of revenge that it is never satisfied; and so, loss and grief lead the woman in black on, trying to exact revenge for her child's accidental death by causing those of others. She cannot let go, and her revenge is an evil that continues to be visited on Crythin Gifford. The grief and craving for revenge must be released or she cannot find resolution and peace on either side of the grave. So here was my central character. Why a 'woman in black'? I must have had Wilkie Collins's *The Woman in White* in mind but it was more than 25 years since I had read his novel. Otherwise, I have no clear idea where she came from.

Thomas Hardy believed that places are as important as people in fiction, because people are formed by the landscapes in which they are born and bred, though that is probably less true now than it was in his day, when, especially in rural areas, they tended to remain rooted in one place. But a harsh climate and a hard landscape toughen people. A low-lying, dank place tends to be lowering to the spirits, and we all know that constant wind drives people mad. I think the pathetic fallacy is less fallacious than is often supposed.

I don't know where the plot of the book came from, partly because I never do know, partly because it is too long ago. But I remember one thing. In the early 1970s I worked by the sea, behind which were the marshes. Walking there at dusk, the light making the dykes gleam and the low wind rattle the reeds, was when I began to think seriously about ghosts.

It seemed natural to adopt a rather formal style and that came along with the point of view. I had to write in the first person. The narrator, Arthur Kipps, is the living key to the book, just as the woman in black is the dead one

POSSESSION

AS BYATT

Possession was, for me, a fortunate book to have written, though at first it appeared to be the opposite. It
was written during two summers when I had just given
up the teaching appointment I had held for 11 years, at
University College London, and it turned out to be the
only one of my novels which was not interrupted by
other problems, projects, illnesses and responsibilities.

I had been thinking about such a novel for at least
15 years, and it had changed a great deal in my head
during that time. Unlike anything else I have written, it
began with the title. I was sitting in the old round reading room in the British Museum, watching the great
Coleridge scholar Kathleen Coburn pacing round and
round the circular catalogue, and I realised that she
had dedicated all her life to this dead man. And then I
thought 'Does he possess her, or does she possess him?'
And then I thought there could be a novel, 'Possession',
about the relations between the living and the dead. It
would be a kind of daemonic tale of haunting.

I then realised that there was a blunt economic
sense to the word. Who 'possesses' the manuscripts of
dead writers? I turned this over in my mind, and quite
a long time later I realised that 'possession' also applied
to sexual relationships. At that time I was working on

the wonderful letters of Robert and Elizabeth Barrett Browning, and I had the idea of two pairs of lovers, one modern, one high Victorian, possessing each other in all these senses.

My original plan had been to write a kind of experimental novel, a ghostly palimpsest of literary, theoretical and intrusively biographical texts, behind which the lovers and poets could be glimpsed, but not seen clearly. What changed everything was my reading of Umberto Eco's *The Name of the Rose*, with its parodic medieval detective story. My husband's friends in the City were all engrossed in this book, and interested in all the medieval theology it contained. The secret, I saw, was that if you tell a strong story, you can include anything else you need to include. So I started inventing a detective story like those I read in my childhood.

I discovered that detective stories have to be constructed backwards – the plot has to be invented to reach a denouement that is already worked out. Things have to be hidden in order to be found at strategic moments. In psychological novels, the characters make the plot as their feelings become clear. The rigour of this new form was a liberation. I found myself parodying scenes from Dorothy L Sayers and Georgette Heyer.

The 'idea' of the novel was that poems have more life than poets, and poems and poets are more lively than literary theorists or biographers living their lives at second hand. I always feel a kind of shock when I turn back to a poet's work after reading things written about him/her. Formally my novel needed the presence of real poems. I don't write poetry. Robertson Davies had written a novel about an opera, and had used the poems of Thomas Lovell Beddoes as a phantom libretto. My editor at the time was that very good (underrated) poet, DJ Enright. I told him I was thinking of using Ezra Pound's early 'Victorian' verses. 'Nonsense,' said Denis. 'You will write them yourself.'

So I went home and wrote a Victorian poem about a spider. I found the poems came easily; they were written as they were needed in the shape of the novel, as part of the run of words – I see a novel as a piece of knitting, all one continuous thread.

People ask me about my 'research', implying that this is a chore, and not the delight of discovering things one didn't know. But in my case I was, and had always been, already possessed by the poems of Tennyson and Browning. I read them as a small child – my mother was a Browning specialist. Their rhythms sing in my head, and indeed crop up oddly in passages of my novels where they are not needed.

When the book was finished, publishers on both sides of the Atlantic were troubled and dubious. They begged me to cut out the poetry, to cut down the Victorian writing. 'You have ruined a nice intrigue with these excrescences,' said the only American publisher brave enough to take it. I wept in the early mornings. Then it won the Irish Times Aer Lingus prize, and the

Booker prize, and to everyone's astonishment – including my own – became a bestseller. People write theses on my imagined poets. It is translated into more than 30 languages. I owe a great deal to Umberto Eco.

THE COUNTRY GIRLS

EDNA O'BRIEN

The Country Girls was my first novel and by far the easiest one to write. True, there was a welter of emotion to be countenanced, but I was happy to be doing it and became lost to the outside world. It had been commissioned by my great supporter Iain Hamilton of Hutchinson and he, in conjunction with Blanche Knopf, paid me a £50 advance, which, true to my profligate nature, I presently spent.

I had read voraciously, loved and sought to learn from writers as disparate as Joyce, Scott Fitzgerald, the Brontës, Flora Thompson, Chekhov, Gogol, Flaubert, Mary Webb, Constance Holme, Colette and Nadine Gordimer. But it was from Ernest Hemingway that I learned the lesson of pruning my prose. Like many fledgling writers, I believed that the merest brush with a published author would somehow crown my garbled efforts. I had moved to London with my husband and children, and when I read that Arthur Michener, an American professor, was giving a talk in a university, I went, to meet the spirit of Hemingway, so to speak. It was an astonishment, a virtual leap, as Michener read the first flawless lines of *A Farewell to Arms*, with such mastery of narrative, imagery and feeling, the prerequisites for great prose.

The Country Girls took three weeks, or maybe less, to write. After I brought my sons Carlo and Sasha to the local school in Morden, I came home, sat by the windowsill of their bedroom and wrote and wrote. It was as if I was merely a medium for the words to flow. The emotional crux hinged on Ireland, the country I had left and wanted to leave, but now grieved for, with an inexplicable sorrow.

Images of roads and ditches and bog and bog lake assailed me, as did the voice of my mother, tender or chastising, and even her cough when she lay down at night. In the fields outside, the lonely plaint of cattle, dogs barking and, as I believed, ghosts. All the people I had encountered kept re-emerging with a vividness: Hickey our workman, whom I loved; my father, whom I feared; knackers; publicans; a travelling salesman by the name of Sacco, who sold spectacles and sets of dentures; and the tinkers who rapped on the door demanding money in exchange for mending tin pots. There was the embryo poet, an amateur historian and the blacksmith who claimed to have met the film director John Ford on the streets of Galway and was asked to appear in *The Quiet Man*, but declined out of filial duty. The lost landscape of childhood.

There was no library in the local town and hence no books. One copy of *Rebecca* had reached us and pages were passed from one woman to the next, though alas not consecutively. Men did not read. Men broke in horses and drove cattle to the fairs and sometimes got drunk and pugilistic.

Where do words come from, I wondered. I still wonder. Because even without books or rather with only prayer books and bloodstock manuals in our house, I had conceived a love of words and assembled my own little crop of them. I believed they had magical associations and that something amazing could be done with them. I had, of course, the language of the Gospels, which to me seemed and seems perfect, and the marvelling narratives of Irish myths and fables. I learned everything through Irish, except English itself, and I loved both tongues.

Before I knew what it meant to be a writer, I had resolved on that path. It was a way out of County Clare. What I did not know was that the homeland was the font from which to draw stories and drama. I now realise that if I had grown up in a city I would not have had such a legacy. That landscape with its beauty and its hardships, its harvests and its hungers was central to my thinking and sensibility.

When I sat down to write the book I did not have to search for a title. It spoke itself – *The Country Girls*. Kate the obedient one, the incurable romantic, and Baba, her alter ego, determined to smash the conventions and defy the strictures of church, priests, nuns and parenthood. I was in a sense both of those girls, though I kept the rebellious side of my nature a secret. My crime, however, did catch up with me.

The novel, published in 1960, caused a bit of consternation. People were outraged. The few copies purchased in Limerick were burnt after the rosary, one evening in the parish grounds, at the request of the priest. I received anonymous letters, all malicious. Then it was banned; nameless gentlemen who sat in some office in Dublin added it to that robust list of novels that were banned in Ireland at that time. Unbeknownst to me, a heated correspondence passed between Archbishop McQuaid of the Dublin diocese, Charles Haughey, then a minister, and the Archbishop of Westminster Cathedral, all deeming it filth, a book that should not be allowed in any decent home. My poor mother was ashamed and had her own private battle with me. She erased with black ink any of the offending words, and the book was put in a bolster case and placed in an outhouse. So much for the glories of publication!

In the big world the reactions were a little chauvinist. Frank O'Connor, in the *New York Times*, concluded that I had appalling taste in men, and LP Hartley, on English television, dismissed it, deeming Baba and Kate a pair of nymphomaniacs. All this a foretaste of judgments to come. I had not at that time read Lord Byron's maxim that a man should calculate on his powers of resistance before entering on a career of writing. I have since read it and must add that a woman embarking on a career of writing needs those powers one hundredfold.

THE BUDDHA OF SUBURBIA

HANIF KUREISHI

From 1979 to 1984, I worked mostly in the theatre – at
the Royal Court, the Soho Poly and the RSC. Then from
1984 to 1987 I wrote the films *My Beautiful Laundrette*
and *Sammy and Rosie Get Laid* for Channel 4. This
made me a bit of money, which meant that I could take
a couple of years out to write some fiction.

I'd written novels throughout my teens, and in
many ways *The Buddha of Suburbia* was the novel that
I'd always been writing. The first half of the novel was
ready to go, while the second half was influenced by the
years I'd spent working in the theatre.

My father was an immigrant, and my family lived
through the first postwar transformation of Britain in
terms of race. Some of that I explored in *My Beautiful
Laundrette*, but there was plenty left over that I wanted
to say. I felt that the period I'd lived through – the
1960s and 70s – was ready to be examined in terms
of race, sex, fashion, drugs and music. I believed that
the novel was the best place for this material as I'd
really be able to stretch out and consider it properly.
But also because it would be a direct method for me –
by which I mean it wasn't mediated through a director
or actors. It was an opportunity for me to find my voice
as a prose writer.

I was also fascinated by the radical politics of the 1970s and became involved with the Workers Revolutionary party, the Communist party and the Socialist Workers party, mainly through my actor friends. I wanted to explore the convolutions of liberals when it came to race. After all pop music, too, turned – often hilariously – towards the Orient as a place of inspiration and nourishment due to the spiritual vacuum of the west – and it was this that I wanted to satirise, this placing of Asians. This is why the father in *The Buddha of Suburbia*, Haroon, is both revered as a mystic and wise man, and spat on as a Paki. If Haroon was alienated in Britain because he was Indian, then his son Karim is alienated in a different way – mainly because people told him he didn't have a place. Bear in mind that I wrote this at a time when society hadn't shifted, hadn't started to see itself as multicultural, so a character like Karim, who was both English and of Indian descent, would be marginalised, placeless.

I think I thought of myself as a British writer, an English writer even; English literature and British sitcoms had been a major influence on me. *The Buddha of Suburbia* therefore gave me the chance to write comedy, which was and is something I enjoy more than anything else – particularly comedy verging on farce, which is especially true of the character of Changez in the novel.

Music is very important in this book, too. It was my obsession when I was growing up, as it was for many people of my generation. This was a time when postwar music was at its best, from the mid-1950s until 1976, just after the beginning of punk. Music was seen by the lower-middle classes as a way of getting out – through art school – into a band. In the novel, Charlie Hero is of course a musician, and he was representative of some of the kids that I grew up with – the Bromley contingent as they were known, including Billy Idol, and the kids who formed Siouxsie and the Banshees and others who became pop photographers or went to work for Vivienne Westwood.

Cyril Connolly once said that if a book you've written is still in print 10 years after it was published, it's an achievement, so at least I've managed that. But I guess also that when *The Buddha of Suburbia*, *My Beautiful Laundrette* and *Midnight's Children* appeared, they opened the door for multiculturalism. Writers who in former times were thought to be marginal began to enter the mainstream. Whereas before you only heard English names, you began to hear Rushdie, Kureishi, Mo, Ishiguro – and it became clear that race and its ramifications were to be the central issue of our time.

THE WASP FACTORY

IAIN BANKS

At the start of 1980 I thought of myself as a science fiction writer, albeit a profoundly unpublished one. I'd wanted to be a writer since primary school and had started trying to write novels when I was 14, finally producing something loosely fitting the definition two years later: a spy story crammed with sex and violence (I still scorn the idea of only writing what you know about). It was written in pencil in an old ship's logbook, and I didn't even bother typing it up; I'd already decided it was juvenilia. The next novel owed something – arguably an apology – to Joseph Heller's *Catch-22* and remains the only book I've ever started without a plan. Lacking a built-in off switch, it tumoured its way to about 400,000 words before I finally got the blighter wrestled to the ground and tied off. That one was typed, and eventually accrued an impressive collection of publishers' rejection slips.

The following three novels, written between 1974 and 1979, were SF, because I'd decided that was what I was: a science fiction writer. It was my genre. I enjoyed the classics and loved contemporary mainstream literature, but I adored science fiction as the exemplary arena of the unfettered imagination, and so that was what I would write, probably for the rest of my career, once I actually had one.

More rejection slips. More rejection slips from a smaller number of publishers, as fewer had SF lists within which to bring my deathless prose to an unsuspecting but, I was certain, ultimately extravagantly appreciative and indeed rightly thankful public.

So by 1980 I was getting fed up. Maybe I wasn't just an SF writer, after all. Maybe I should try writing an ordinary, boring, mainstream novel. Maybe it was even time to consider writing a second draft of one of these works of patent genius, rather than trusting that London publishers would have the wit to recognise an obvious rough diamond which, a trifling number of easily polished awkwardnesses having been dealt with, was surely about to make the ungrateful wretches millions. . .

The Wasp Factory represented me admitting partial defeat, heaving a slightly theatrical sigh, stepping reluctantly away from the gaudy, wall-size canvases of science/space fiction to lay down my oversize set of Rolf Harris paint rollers, pick up a set of brushes thinner than pencils and – jaw set, brows furrowed – lower myself to using a more restricted palette and to producing what felt like a miniature in comparison.

I'd grown up in Fife and Gourock/Greenock; I suppose I could have attempted some piece of gnarly Scots realism. I'd been to university; I might have gone for a student campus novel. I'd not long moved to London so could have essayed a Bumpkin in the Big, Bad City book.

In the end I went for something that kept me closer to my by-then comfort zone: a first-person narrative set on a remote Scottish nearly-island told by a normality-challenged teenager with severe violence issues allowed me to treat my story as something resembling SF. The island could be envisaged as a planet, and Frank, the protagonist, almost as an alien. I gave in to the write-what-you-know school but with a dose of skiffy hyperbole, mining my own past for exaggerateable experiences. I'd built dams; Frank would too, though with a slightly psychotic über-motif involving women, water, the sea and revenge. I'd constructed big home-made kites; so would Frank, and use one as a murder weapon. Along with a pal, I'd indulged in the then not-uncommon and perfectly innocent teenage boy pursuit of making bombs, flame-throwers, guns, giant cata-pults and more bombs; Frank would too, though alone and with a more determinedly harm-minded intensity.

Beyond that, it was supposed to be a pro-feminist, antimilitarist work, satirising religion and comment-ing on the way we're shaped by our surroundings and upbringing and the usually skewed information we're presented with by those in power. Frank is supposed to stand for all of us, in some ways: deceived, misled, harking back to something that never existed, venge-ful for no good reason and trying too hard to live up to some oversold ideal that is of no real relevance, anyway. There are places, too, where I was trying to use Frank to express something about the stated and real reasons for brutality (hence Frank's musings on the attack on the rabbit warren).

I was also trying to make the point that childhood innocence isn't – and wasn't – as most people seem to imagine it: children probably harbour quite as many violent thoughts as adults, they just don't usually possess a sophisticated moral framework within which to place them.

Not, come to think of it, that all adults do, either.

COLD MOUNTAIN

CHARLES FRAZIER

I've never been very attached to genre labels and never set out intentionally to write historic fiction. Besides, what you consider historic depends on how far back your memory extends.

From my childhood, I remember a tiny old woman named Mary, made pale and almost translucent by time. Mary's childhood memories extended back to the confusing and violent finale of the civil war, and she told stories of brutal murders in those days and refused to name some of the killers, as if dead men might still be prosecuted in the late 1950s. So, just one direct transmission of memory from hers to mine makes for a pretty shallow past. And yet, the civil war is as mythic in the American mind as the siege of Troy.

The year I began *Cold Mountain*, 1989, I had been working on a novel set in the current moment. About all I recall clearly of those months of writing is a beautiful couple of September weeks in Jackson Hole, Wyoming, and a story set in the southern Appalachians and in northern Mexico, Tarahumara country, where I'd spent some time. I recall a hapless narrator on the road trying to find his runaway wife. But by late fall that year I had abandoned the story because I had fallen into a much better one, and it just happened to be historic.

As I wrote my way into it, I found myself less and less interested in the civil war itself, all that fetishising of the generals and their tragic grandeur. I was more interested in the devastation visited on ordinary lives. And also the shadows it cast forward to the present, since it has always seemed to me that historic novels tell as much about the times in which they are written as the times in which they are set.

I was interested, too, in why my ancestors volunteered to fight. They didn't own slaves; like most people, they did their own work. Of four brothers, two were dead by the time General Robert E Lee handed over his sword and went home to brood and fade into such a legend that even his horse has its own large grave marker. My great-great grandfather was one of the surviving brothers. He came back and built a small country chapel – still standing – and became a Universalist minister.

I wished I had been able to ask him how he looked at the war when he volunteered and how he looked at it when he came home. So, the story I found myself writing became an *Odyssey*, not an *Iliad*. Returning, not going. A long journey home through a devastated world. Late in the third century BC, the Greek geographer Eratosthenes wrote: 'You will find the scene of the wanderings of Odysseus when you find the cobbler who sewed up the bag of the four winds.' His point, of course, had to do with readers who get twisted up trying to untangle fact and fiction, especially the ones needing too much of the former.

While writing *Cold Mountain*, I held maps of two geographies, two worlds, in my mind as I wrote. One was an early map of North Carolina. Overlaying it, though, was an imagined map of the landscape Jack travels in the southern Appalachian folktales. He's much the same Jack who climbs the beanstalk, vulnerable and clever and opportunistic. Also sometimes violent. The mountains he wanders seem to go on forever. I wanted *Cold Mountain* to incorporate the sort of practical magic and weirdness of those stories and of murder ballads and lonesome fiddle tunes, but I also wanted the book to insist on the reality of its fictional world.

Henry James wrote that 'The historical novel is, for me condemned ... to a fatal cheapness.' And yet he also wrote that 'The sense of the past is our sense.' I kept both of those lines pinned to the wall over my writing desk. Every day, trying to avoid the one and reach for the other. It is not either/or, though. It's a continuum. *The Scarlet Pimpernel* near one end, *The Scarlet Letter* near the other.

I had never taken creative writing classes. Hadn't even considered it. So the first couple of years were a learning process. Just simple things, like understanding the narrative voice as a distinct character in the book. Certainly not me and also not the characters' inner voices, but the voice of the tale teller with his/her distinct language and knowledge and attitude toward the world. Maybe I would have learned that in the first week of a creative writing programme, but to me fiction seems too important to professionalise. Leave it to amateurs. You're always in the process of learning the trade anyway, even though it's a primitive one, shaped from fragile materials, mostly just words and memory.

...✐

SMALL ISLAND

ANDREA LEVY

I hadn't realised I was starting a novel. I thought I was just being curious about my own family history when, in my 40s, I finally got my mum to tell me about her experiences of emigrating from Jamaica to Britain. She always claimed that I was never interested in her past when I was younger. But the way I remember it, neither she nor my dad ever seemed to want to talk about their lives in Jamaica, or about why in 1948 they made the momentous decision to leave that island to come to another. Whatever the truth, that silence was finally breached and my mother, reluctantly, began to speak to me about her life before I was born. I was gripped from the start as those two familiar parents of mine began to emerge as fully rounded human beings with an amazing story to tell.

My dad had died in the 1980s, but I remember him mentioning, almost in passing, that he had sailed to this country on a ship called the *Empire Windrush*. Over the next decade or so the name of that ship kept cropping up – in TV documentaries, books, newspaper articles. By the mid-1990s there was even talk of the '*Windrush* generation'. The arrival of that ship in 1948, with its 492 West Indian migrants looking for work and betterment in the mother country, had become an important moment in our recent history – a point at which British society began to change. And he was one of the pioneers. My dad!

I wanted to explore the relationship that the Caribbean islands had with Britain. After all it was no accident, no sticking a pin in a map, that brought my parents here. It was a legacy of the British empire. My parents believed themselves to be British. They really thought they would be welcomed here. They really did get a shock.

But throughout my mum's story of arriving in England, she would talk about the white English people she met. Some she dismissed with a wave of her hand, but others she would talk of fondly. That they helped her, and made an impact on her, was clear. I realised if I was going to tell this story I had to tell it from all sides. Not only the immigrants' tale, but also from the point of view of the people that those immigrants came to live among. Their lives were changed by that migration to Britain just as my parents' lives were.

I had also been talking to my mother-in-law about her childhood. She had grown up in the 1920s and 30s on a farm in the East Midlands. Those conversations became very important in forming Queenie's back-story. In my mother-in-law's conversations she talked about her husband, who died in the 1960s and who I never met. He had been in the RAF in Burma during the second world war. I suddenly realised what a catalyst the war must have been. That conflict was barely over when my parents arrived in bombed-out London.

I was also struck by how much my parents and my parents-in-law would have had in common despite the obvious difference of the colour of their skin. What would have happened if by some chance they could have met at that time? Would they have been able to discover this common ground? That's when I began to imagine four people – two white English, two black Jamaican – in a rundown house in Earls Court in 1948. What happened to them to bring them to that place and time? And what would they think of each other?

So the book was started. At first I was very nervous writing a totally researched book. Unlike my previous novels I was venturing out of my own experience and into another world. But it became so fascinating that the fears disappeared. I read books, old newspapers, visited archives and museums, watched films. I talked to war veterans and people who had lived through those times. I immersed myself in the period I was writing about, the speech, the attitudes, even the music and the styles of dress. It was such fun. Four distinct characters began to form in my head, and all of them seemed to demand that they tell their own stories. So four first-person narratives became the structure of the novel. And as I explored their stories I came to better understand the relationship between the country of my birth and the country of my heritage. *Small Island* was a joy to write and those characters will stay with me forever. It became a work of fiction, but for me it still remains something of a family history, too.

...✒

UNSEEN ACADEMICALS

TERRY PRATCHETT

In the nature of things, readers are often moved to suggest 'topics' for my Discworld books. This is somewhat depressing, because most people who are not writers fail to understand how writers think, and if it comes to that, so do I.

Regrettably, football is often on the metaphorical wish list. People don't always realise that a plot is only one of the things that a book needs, and one of the other things is a point. I couldn't see the point of writing a novel about football, a game I have never watched and, when at school, avoided like the plague; I was generally last to be picked before the fat kid. (We came into our own one year, however, when we did hockey. That meant I had a stick and lots of advice from my father, who had learned how to cheat at hockey in India, and even the fat kid found a new, well-padded role as a goalie.)

But, like many authors, I research serendipitously, and I enjoy reading about the social history of Victorian England. I came across a little anecdote about the man who invented the pneumatic football, without which the modern game could not possibly exist. I was sufficiently intrigued to look a bit further, and into my head came the phrase 'two supporters' clubs, alike in villainy'. And within half an hour, four major characters were alive in my head and down on the page. The speed at which the rest of the book was created around them was some kind of tribute, I suppose, to a lifetime's writing.

Generally speaking, if you get your characters right, they will in some way 'speak for themselves'. In *Unseen Academicals*, the prime example of this is Glenda.

Initially, I had seen Glenda as playing the nurse role in this football-flavoured version of *Romeo and Juliet*. In a way, of course, she does, flapping around after her young friend, as my father would put it, like an old hen. But the book really began to take shape for me when she began to think outside the little box of her life. I have known many women like her; they mucked around at school, got married and had some kids, and then realised that they had a fully functional brain, often fearsomely so. They usually find a voice then, as well. Glenda does so, to the extent of barging in to Lord Vetinari's office like an angry mum besieging the headmaster after her little boy has had a telling off. I rather like her, ever since I realised that she didn't know the meaning of some of the more worrying words in the cheap romantic novels she bought, and was ashamed at her lack of knowledge.

Mr Nutt was in a way the seed of the book. Ever since I first read Tolkien at the age of 13, I was worried about the orcs. They were totally and irrevocably bad. It was a flat given. No possibility of redemption for an orc, no chance of getting a job somewhere involving fluffy animals or flowers.

This is no reflection on Tolkien. We are all prisoners in the aspic of our time. But now, I think, people have learned not to think that any race or culture is naturally or irredeemably bad. We have seen the world from space and it isn't flat.

I have waited decades to write about Nutt; I can remember the excesses of football hooliganism that began in the 1960s and have only recently been cleaned up. It was a world of scaffolding-pole clubs and Stanley knives slashing railway seats and faces. The orcs, with a scarf or two, would have fitted right in in those days. More recently, an inflatable banana is the worst thing that's brandished; it would appear that the leopard can change his shorts.

And, of course, as this is a Discworld book, it means that the wizards have to find something to squabble about. Mr Dibbler must try a new scam, Lord Vetinari must plot, in his Machiavellian way, towards a better world, and boy must meet girl or at least drift gently towards her.

Over the years I have endeavoured to keep the Discworld series fresh for the long-time fans as well as for the newcomers. I believe that *Unseen Academicals* must be among the more accessible. Indeed, it contains so little of what is popularly thought of as fantasy that in some places it comes close to that strange creature known as magical realism. Various factors made it somewhat difficult to write, and like every book I have ever written, I wish I could have given it a fortnight of extra time, but the editor's whistle was about to blow, so I had to take the shot.

...🖋

THE MILLSTONE

MARGARET DRABBLE

The Millstone was my third novel and I wrote it while I was expecting my third baby. Its subject, not surprisingly, is maternity. There weren't many novels about maternity in those days, but I don't think I had any sense of entering forbidden or dangerous ground. I was writing about what was all around me, the daily lives of myself and my friends, the struggle to work and bring up children at the same time. Those were the days of the *Guardian* women's page, under the legendary Mary Stott, when it was a forum for discussions about playgroups and separation anxiety, breastfeeding and vaccination and other less womanly topics. I used to write for it occasionally, and knew there was a companionable readership out there, although I was often lonely at home, as young mothers are.

I wrote novels to keep myself company, and with my first book had discovered an informal first-person narrative voice that took me by surprise. It seemed to arrive from nowhere, and I stayed with it for my first three books. I had liberated myself from the neutral critical prose of the university essay (which I had greatly enjoyed writing) and found a new way of exploring the non-literary world. The protagonist of *The Millstone* is an aspiring academic, and part of me wished

I had become one too, but she is more concerned with her illegitimate baby than with finishing her thesis. I don't know how consciously I isolated her experience of motherhood by making her an unmarried mother, which obviated the necessity of dealing either with marriage or with a male father figure. I must have had reasons for this, but am still not sure what they were. It wasn't a literary decision.

The illness of the child sprang directly from personal experience. One of my children had been diagnosed with a heart lesion, or hole in the heart, and Rosamund's anxieties were very much my own. She was braver than I, but I did have a sense of writing on behalf of many mothers as she confronted hospital authority. I dramatised my predicament, as writers do, but I didn't think that dishonest. The issue was real, and I think my treatment of it was useful. I didn't realise until many years later that some of the medical details I invented were way off the mark. I would do that differently now, and the story would be more painful.

In terms of the literary history, I was becoming aware in the 1960s that the woman's novel, always strong in England, was moving in new directions, driven by a changing educational system and changing opportunities. The courtship novel of Fanny Burney and Jane Austen was giving way to the post-courtship novel of marital conflict and professional ambitions. Feminist criticism was slowly bringing our attention to the fact that nearly all the great women writers of the past were childless. Elizabeth Gaskell, or Mrs Gaskell as we called her, was an exception, and so was the undervalued Mary Shelley. (We never called her Mrs Shelley.) My contemporaries and I were working in a strong female tradition, but in an age of double values and contradictory expectations, and you can see the stress in Sylvia Plath, Doris Lessing, Edna O'Brien and Nell Dunn, whose work I was discovering at this time – though I hadn't read any of them when I first embarked on writing fiction. My living role models then were Angus Wilson and Saul Bellow.

I wasn't thinking about literary history when I wrote *The Millstone*. I was writing to exorcise fear, I was writing for luck, I was writing in hope. There are bits of the novel I regret, moments of unwitting snobbery and self-conscious smartness. But Rosamund was what she was, she was of her age, caught at the opening of an era that she didn't know how to enter – on the border between the one-night stand of the ignorant virgin and the one-night stand of Bridget Jones. The sexual ignorance of the young in those days was remarkable. So was the sexual ignorance of the old. My publisher's reader (a man, and middle aged) queried the plot, on the grounds that it was almost impossible to get pregnant during the first act of intercourse.

After *The Millstone*, I stopped writing first-person novels. I came to think it a lazy form, and embarked on more complex and ambitious polyphonic efforts. I sometimes wish I could recapture that easy single linear narrative, and in *The Seven Sisters* in 2002 I tried to do so, but felt mysteriously compelled to mess it up with a bit of modish postmodernism. Modish postmodernism was easy. It's the straight true line that's hard.

...✐

THE RELUCTANT FUNDAMENTALIST

MOHSIN HAMID

I've always had problems with borders. Maybe it's because the place I call home keeps changing. Or maybe it's what causes me to keep changing the place I call home. I'm not sure.

Either way, the basic itinerary of my life has been this: born in Lahore, moved to San Francisco at age three, to Lahore again at nine, to New Jersey at 18, to Lahore a third time at 22, to Boston at 23, New York at 26, London at 30, and Lahore a fourth time at 38. (I've had multi-month stints in Manila and Milan as well.)

When I travel, I feel more like a nomad than a tourist. In Istanbul to give a lecture last week, I wasn't dreaming of the next meal or next sight. I was dreaming of moving there. It was the same when I visited Tokyo. And Paris. And Cairo. And Santiago. And Sydney. I've had a lifelong love affair with Lahore, but it's been far from monogamous. I'm constantly flirting with other cities.

As a kid I read widely: comics, science fiction, news magazines, children's books, atlases, 'literature'. But I never really understood the boundaries between genres. For me, *Charlotte's Web* was as profound a meditation on mortality as *The Death of Ivan Ilyich*.

I also never really understood the boundary between the roles of character and reader. Often, when I read, I felt like the character I was reading about. So I was drawn to the role-playing game Dungeons and Dragons, where players create imaginary personas and sally forth into mutually conceived worlds of swords and sorcery. And I was fascinated by the *Choose Your Own Adventure* series of books ('Of you step out of the time capsule, go to page 22; if you try to fix the mission computer, go to page 41').

As I evolved as a writer, from navel-high producer of galactic space operas to fuzz-sprouting fantasist imagining nonexistent island countries, to university dabbler in more or less realistic short stories to twentysomething unpublished novelist, I became more and more interested in the interactive nature of fiction.

I began to wonder if the power of the novel, if its distinctive feature among contemporary mass-story-telling forms, was rooted in the enormous degree of co-creation it requires on the part of its audience. (After all, when you watch a film or TV show, what you see looks like what it represents; when you read a novel, what you see is black ink on pulped wood, and it is you who projects scenes on to the screen of your imagination.)

If the novel was special because it allowed writers and readers to create jointly, to dance together, then it seemed to me that I should try to write novels that maximised this possibility of opening themselves up to being read in different ways, to involving the reader as a kind of character, indeed as a kind of co-writer.

I wasn't sure how to do this. I spent seven years writing my first novel, *Moth Smoke*, trying to figure it out. I found lessons in Calvino. I found lessons in *Pulp Fiction*. I wrote it again and again. Slowly, *Moth Smoke* morphed into a trial. You, the reader, were cast as the judge. You would be given the ex-banking, pot-smoking, heroin-addicted, love-struck narrator's story. You would be given the counter-stories of his best friend, his sexy lover, and his possible partner in crime. You would be given legal memos on, for example, the role of air conditioning in the lives of the main characters. And you would be asked to decide.

Moth Smoke became a bestseller in Pakistan and India. Encouraged, I thought my second novel would be easier. I was wrong. *The Reluctant Fundamentalist* took me seven years as well. I completed the first draft in July 2001, a wistful account of a young Pakistani working in corporate New York who, after a failed love affair, grows a beard and moves back to Lahore. It was terrible, as my first drafts always are. My job is to write a book increasingly less badly over time.

A few weeks later, the terrorist attacks of September 11 happened. My world changed. I wrote the novel again. And again. I wrote it in the first person. I wrote it in the third person. I wrote it as a fable. I wrote it in an American accent. It just refused to work.

I looked to Camus for inspiration, and to *High Noon*. Eventually I arrived at what I hoped was an appropriately catalysing voice, a voice modelled on class-conscious graduates of elite Pakistani schools (set up by the British a century and a half ago), which, in its formal rigidity and potential menace and sense of hailing from the past, chimed stylistically with certain popular stereotypes about Muslims and Islam.

And I also arrived at what I hoped was an appropriately permeable form, a dramatic monologue, a half-conversation spoken to 'you' that leaves it to the reader to supply its missing context. So readers end up creating their own versions of what happens in the book, and the book in turn moves and shifts and reflects in response to the individual inclinations and world views of readers.

For me, writing a novel is like solving a puzzle. But I don't intend my novels as puzzles. I intend them as invitations to dance.

GENERATION X

DOUGLAS COUPLAND

It's a Sunday afternoon and 20 years since I sat down to begin writing *Generation X*. And it feels like 20 years, too – no *tempus fugit* for me.

And it's odd that *Gen X* was the thing that would change my life, because everything about the book reeked of disaster and bad decision-making. I'd only begun writing less than three years earlier – non-fiction for magazines in Canada – and I was soon hitting that point in life where poor decisions come back to bite one. I was at the end of my 20s and it was becoming clear to me that my 30s were going to be a continuing mix of rootlessness and poverty.

Then, in 1989, a hotshot Toronto agent sold the idea of *Generation X* to both a Canadian and an American publisher. The agent was a real huckster, and the book he promised the publishers was supposed to be a field guide to a post-boomer sensibility. One must remember that in 1989, nobody believed that there was a post-boomer sensibility.

The advance was enough for me to quit freelancing for a small while to focus on the book. But then, one afternoon in April of 1989, I was emerging from the Davisville subway station – there had just been a rainstorm and the sunset was cold and tangerine – and a wave swept over me, one of those waves that occur not too often in one's lifetime. It was one of the few times I've ever heard 'a voice' (whatever a voice really is), and the voice very clearly said to me: 'OK, Doug. It appears that you're going to be a full-time writer now. Good. But that means you have to write fiction rather than non-fiction, because fiction is purer. You'll have to clear all your decks and you're going to have to change the way you see both you and your future.'

And then the voice left, and I was just another guy standing on a wet sidewalk outside the Golden Griddle. But life was now different.

I foolishly took out a lease on a tiny bungalow in Palm Springs, California, for no other reason than that I'd been there once before and it seemed like a romantic place to write a book – oh, the naivety of youth. And by locking myself into a lease in the State of California I'd shackled myself to a year of profound loneliness and despair, the grimness of which haunts me to this day. This was 1989, and Palm Springs had yet to become hip or gay, or trendy, or a good real-estate investment. It was a bell jar of a (by then) astonishingly geriatric way of life that had calcified around 1964. I was the only person under the age of 45 in the Coachella Valley (now the home of a genuinely hip music festival, which seems amazing to me. In 1989, the acme of Palm Springs hipness was a deli on Tahquitz Canyon Drive that sold coffee until its 8pm closing time). It was truly madness to move to the middle of nowhere, to write fiction – I'd never written fiction – and some-how assume things would work out. Ah, youth and its protective coating of cluelessness.

And so I started to write the book. I remember spending my days almost dizzy with loneliness and feeling like I'd sold the family cow for three beans. I suppose it was this crippling loneliness that gave *Gen X* its bite. I was trying to imagine a life for myself on paper that certainly wasn't happening in reality. In the book there was the idea that people marooned in life could unmaroon themselves by telling stories to each other. That still seems to me to be a valid way of seeing the world. There was also the notion that telling stories was a way of coping with information overload – hence the book's subtitle, *Tales for an Accelerated Culture*. In 1989, information overload meant 50 TV stations instead of 10, as well as push-button phones instead of rotary dial phones – quaint now, but back then it felt real. What was really going on with the writing of *X* was, I suspect, the use of storytelling as a form of crea-tive pattern recognition from which clues to psychic survival might erupt. That's possibly what storytelling is in a large sense, and it's what I do for a living, the most recent evidence of which is *Generation A*, a follow-up to *X* where the cultural acceleration experienced by the characters is palpable rather than theoretical.

In any event, I FedEx'd the manuscript to New York and Toronto on 1 April, and then began to wait and wait and wait and wait for a response. None came. By summer the temperature was around 110 degrees every day, and my landlord kindly let me out of my lease and, being broke and Canadian, I moved to Montreal, a city where being broke and Canadian at least had some dimension of flair. By midsummer I learned that the Canadians had rejected the book outright (I have a weirdly snippy letter from them somewhere) and the US publishers were going to delay the book indefinitely. Boy, talk about giving a young writer self-esteem issues. My good fortune was that the younger staff at the US publisher became vocal in their demand that the book be published, which occurred ever so grudgingly in March of 1991. A chewed-up plastic courier bag holding two mangled copies of the book arrived in Montreal, and looking at them I noticed that its cover didn't actually cover the pages, which stuck out maybe ¼ inch from the edge. When I asked my editor what were they thinking, I was told not to be so picky.

Welcome to the overnight and highly charmed success story of *Generation X*.

It worked out in the end, but I still have dreams where I don't know what I do for a living and wake up in a panic. And I still wonder what might have happened to that painfully skinny, strangely clueless Doug who moved off to the desert in 1989, a parallel-universe Doug whose publishers never did, in the end, publish his book. Where would he be now? Would he be happy or sad or lost? I think of that Doug many times every day of my life, and when I write books now, it's that other Doug who is my audience of one, not me.

QUARANTINE

JIM CRACE

Despite what many of my readers and critics might believe, I am a cheerful optimist, both on the page and off it. But unwarranted optimism – of the kind that promises non-sinners an eternity of heaven, for example, or suggests, Hollywood-style, that virtue (and beauty!) will normally be rewarded with good fortune – I find to be both fraudulent and harmful. My own optimism is atheistic and, I hope, less cynical. It accepts that we all live finite lives in an implacable, unfair, probably infinite universe, but celebrates that despite the heavy troubles and the dark places we might encounter during our three-score years and 10 we are lucky to be here at all. It has been in those dark places that my fiction has sought to establish its tough optimism.

One such dark and troubled place during the late 1980s was the rambling hotel at the top of our street in the Birmingham suburb of Moseley. Under the Thatcherite money-snatching policy of 'Care in the Community', the building had been converted into a hostel for patients with mental health problems. In this case, as a television report revealed, there was little or no care in the community but plenty of squalor, neglect and overcrowding. I had the chance one morning to sneak into its corridors. Here were dozens of cell-like rooms, hardly large enough to stretch your arms, occupied by a community of depressives, addicts and obsessives with little in common except their current despair. This I thought – in my cheerful, optimistic manner – would make an engrossing subject for a novel: how does a community of people, all living on the edge, secure some comfort, resolution and transcendence in what I considered to be a godless universe?

If I had been a realist I could, of course, have set the novel in Thatcher's Britain and simply held a mirror up to what was happening less than half a mile from my own home. But I do not have photographic skills as a writer. I am a fabulist, more attracted to metaphor than reportage. So the idea was left to brew for several years, until one day my metaphor dropped through the letterbox. It was a postcard sent by some friends visiting Jericho in Palestine. It showed the Mount of Temptation where the historical Jesus was reputed to have spent his 40 days rebuffing the advances of the Devil before embarking on his ministry. Yet there were many man-made, cell-like caves in the crumbling hill-side, not just the one that Jesus would have needed. It occurred to me that possibly at that time anyone who had a problem, any depressive, addict or obsessive, not just the aspirant Son of God, might have taken to these caves to battle with their demons. It would have been a community of people living on the edge: an ancient version of my Moseley hostel, in other words. I flipped the postcard over and read the name of the Mount in

Latin-inflected Arabic: Jebel Quruntul, the Hill of 40 Days, the Hill of Quarantine. I had my title for the book. I had my metaphor. Now I could begin.

But books – if they are going well – have the habit of shaking off this author and his first intentions, of setting and insisting on unforeseen agendas of their own. I can remember very well the afternoon that *Quarantine* abandoned me and my intended satire of Thatcherism and went off on a tangent. It was the passage when Jesus was meant to make a brief guest appearance. He'd be allowed half a sentence at the most, and only to give my chosen setting its historical provenance. I wrote. 'He was a traveller called Jesus, from the cooler farming valleys in the north. . .' But that half-line expanded into a paragraph, and that paragraph bloated into a chapter, and that chapter offered up a host of possibilities. By tea-time, the traveller had seemed to cure – with a miracle? – a satanic man called Musa. Jesus was unignorable now. He would become a major character.

'Ah, that's because the Holy Ghost was standing at your shoulder while you wrote,' I was subsequently assured by a fellow guest (a priest) on a radio show.

No, not the Holy Ghost, I said, but the Imp of Storytelling, celebrated for its mischievousness, its cunning, and its generosity. It had caused me, an atheist, intent on writing a novel broadly about contemporary earthly matters, to produce a book of strangely scriptural intensity, a novel that (mostly) underscored people's faith in gods rather than undermined it.

I was surprised and elated when I finished writing *Quarantine* by how thoroughly I had been abandoned by the narrative and how exalted its tone and ambition had become. I am surprised by it still, as – ever the optimist – I always expect to be surprised with any book. I write. And I am grateful to the Imp for that.

NOTES ON A SCANDAL

ZOË HELLER

At some point during the summer of 2000, I had an idea of writing a novel about a love affair between a woman teacher and her teenaged pupil. The infamous Mary Kay Letourneau case had recently been in the US news, and a lot of things about that story had intrigued me – not least the amount of journalistic cant it inspired on the subject of female sexuality and 'appropriate' sexual relationships. The line that I had in mind when I began writing – the motto for the book, in a way – was one of WH Auden's: 'The desires of the heart are as crooked as corkscrews.'

I made a number of false starts with the book – writing it from the teacher's point of view, from an omniscient, third-person perspective and so on – until, a couple of months in, it occurred to me to tell the story in the voice of Barbara, an older colleague and friend of the badly behaved teacher. Philip Roth once described novel-writing as a process of 'problem-solving', and for me, the discovery of Barbara offered a solution to several problems all at once. It was a great 'Aha!' moment. I felt straight away that I knew Barbara inside out, that I 'had' her voice. It was one of those rare instances in my writing life when I was positively eager to get to the computer and start work every day. Perhaps the most useful thing that Barbara gave me was a way of opening the book up and complicating things. Suddenly I had a new way of showing love's crooked ways, but I also had a weird, charismatic narrator, and a new range of Barbara-related subjects – childlessness, loneliness, old age – to write about.

One often hears critics praise particular novelists for being 'in control' of their material – by which they mean, I suppose, that the novelists in question have marshalled their themes and characters and so on, in a confident, surefooted way. As a writer, though, I am wary of feeling too in control. If I know exactly what I'm doing and what a book is 'saying' at any given moment, the chances are the thing I'm writing will be dead on the page. Ideally, I want to feel as if I'm oversee-ing a big, unruly classroom and only just managing to keep order.

It took me two years to finish *Notes* – I am a patheti-cally slow writer – and during that time, I showed it to no one but my husband. When I finally sent it out to publishers, I received what is politely known as a 'mixed' response. My loyal editor at Viking, Juliet Annan, made an offer on it, but seven or eight publish-ers in the US rejected it. And I received an awful reader's report from somewhere that ended with the heartbreaking line: 'With a lot of work, this could be a quite interesting book – but only quite.'

Many of the first readers objected to what they saw as Barbara's unmitigated unpleasantness. Several people expressed the view that 'there was no one to like' in the book. I was then – and I remain – unsure how to answer these complaints. Part of me feels that I have failed if I have not managed to conjure any sympathy for my flawed, difficult characters. And part of me feels that the complaining readers are the ones at fault for bringing to fiction misplaced expectations of finding 'nice people'.

Happily, *Notes* went on to find a publisher in the US, although, rather maddeningly, it ended up being published under another title: *What Was She Thinking?* (I hated the idea of giving the book two different English-language titles, but the Americans were adamant that *Notes on a Scandal* sounded like a non-fiction book about the Clinton presidency.)

Looking back now on some of the early, unfavourable responses to the book, I suspect that they had a rather salutary effect on me. Having your work occasionally rejected – or poorly reviewed – is not a bad thing for a writer. Naturally, it's horrid at the time, but it does toughen you up. It also forces you to decide whether you're in the game for the long haul or not.

TRAINSPOTTING

IRVINE WELSH

Trainspotting was the book I had to do, basically to get it out of the way, in order to become a writer. I had been obsessed with books and literature for a while, and having failed at everything else, thought that I could give writing a go. But I had to understand my own personal journey and the issues I had come through first. What sort of a person was I? What could I bring to this? I knew that I could never do genre fiction; I wouldn't have the ability to write into a marketing hole. It would bore me to tears and be too much like the proper jobs I hated. It had to be about me expressing myself, without recourse to formulae.

When I looked at my notes and doodlings in diaries over the years, I didn't have much to bring to the table. My life was essentially defined by, at best, mediocrity (I had risen to middle-management level in the public sector), and at worst failure. This latter element was with reference to recurrent drug issues, which have been discussed at length elsewhere. So I decided that this would be my starting point.

Far more important than either, I'd always been blessed with a rich inner life. I had a very happy child-hood, but it always seemed a precarious one, due to the ongoing illness of one of my parents. It often seemed easier to retreat into my own head rather than deal with what was going on around me. I recall a report card at school saying that I would 'never amount to anything' as I was 'too much of a dreamer'. This was meant as scornful condemnation; even at the time I instinctively felt it was positive and it provided me with a great deal of affirmation. For such a child, a book is a godsend. Sitting with one in front of me gave me permission to dream and enriched and defined my creative landscape.

But becoming a writer was something I didn't consider, even though one English teacher had told me that I should. Instead I found myself on the City and Guilds electronics technician course at Telford College, Edinburgh, trying to get a trade. Writing was seen as something that the idle rich did. The consensus was that working-class people read recreationally – they didn't have the time to learn the craft of the writer. This, of course, is self-defeating nonsense, but it was reinforced by the lives of my first literary heroes, people like Evelyn Waugh.

My uncle Jack was a fireman who was doing an Open University course and he passed on his books to my father. Through this avenue Waugh's *Sword of Honour* trilogy came into my possession. This was a revelation to me. I loved his prose and his way of setting out relationships between his characters; that odd mixture of respect and rivalry, love and contempt, was to be a huge influence on my own writing. I recognised the people around me in the type of relationships he mapped out.

But the problem was that he wasn't like me or the people around me. He was a toff. So I went on a search, from Russian classics to Black American writing, to try to find a voice and set of social circumstances that chimed. I found it back home in Ayrshire when I picked up a copy of William McIlvaney's *Docherty*. Then came James Kelman's *The Busconductor Hines* and Alasdair Gray's *Lanark*.

But these experiences seemed to be arguments against Thatcherite capitalism, while I thought, even then, that this argument was essentially nostalgic. I believed that social changes and the forces of the time made it inevitable that 'they' would win the class war. Yes, this irked me as an individual, and I went on all the pickets and demonstrations, through the miners' strike onwards, but to do the right thing rather than in anticipation of victory. What I was concerned about was the social landscape we'd be left with after this: baldly, the substitution of drugs for jobs in the poorest parts of Britain.

So I started to write *Trainspotting*, as a way of making sense of my own life and times. When I wrote the book I was living in different circumstances from the characters in it. I had a good job, was married, and largely had my substance abuse issues under control. Acid house knocked me out of this comfort zone. Soon I was back out tearing it up at the weekends, energised by the power of that scene, but also with a new-found reflectiveness that the ecstasy 'comedowns' exacerbated.

I knocked out a draft from old notes and diaries. It was way too long – about 250,000 words. I just chopped the ends off, and wrote a (I thought fairly cheesy) heist ending, in order to finish the book. I thought it would never be published, but the first person I sent it to took it on. I don't know how many languages it's been translated into or how much it has sold worldwide, but it has cast a big shadow and I've resigned myself to being called '*Trainspotting* author Irvine Welsh' for the rest of my life, even though I've written better books and will hopefully continue to do so. I just know that for the last decade a big grin has split my face twice a year when the royalty cheque hits the doormat. So being 'the *Trainspotting* guy' isn't so bad.

RIDDLEY WALKER

RUSSELL HOBAN

People say to me: 'Where do you get your ideas?' 'Out of the air,' I tell them. This is a fact, though not a simple one. The air is different in different places; it is the local atmosphere, the medium through which pass the history of the place and the ideas there indwelling.

The first time I stood in Canterbury Cathedral and tilted my head back to look up, up, up to that numinous fan-vaulting I felt the uprush past me of all the centuries of prayer, of hope and fear and yearning, yearning for answers and, if possible, salvation.

Breathing in this atmosphere I made my way through the nave to those stone steps trodden by successive waves of pilgrims, some with beads, some with cameras. Up those worn-down steps, past the place where the remembered blood of Thomas Becket seethes on the stones, to the north aisle where on one wall remains the faint earth-green tracery of *The Legend of St Eustace*. Facing it on the opposite wall is Professor Tristram's reconstruction of the 15th-century painting.

Whatever talent I have for writing lies in being friends with my head: I know its vagaries, its twists and turns, its hobo journeys in fast freights, riding the blinds to unknown destinations. Sometimes I get thrown off the train in the middle of nowhere; sometimes I get to the

Big Rock Candy Mountain. If you Google for Eustace you'll find that he has no official standing among the beatified. Perhaps his legend turned up on the back of some Middle-Ages cornflakes box and grew from there. Being thus non-factual, Eustace is quite at home in a work of fiction. According to the legend he was a general in the Roman army to begin with, but one day hunting in the forest, he saw a little crucified Jesus between the antlers of a stag, as vividly shown in the 15th-century painting by Pisanello.

This epiphany brought him to his knees and converted him to Christianity. He set out with his wife and their two little sons on a pilgrimage to Jerusalem and this painting by an unknown artist shows, vertically from bottom to top, the ill-starred journey from beginning to end: Eustace's wife is taken by pirates early on, leaving Eustace to soldier on with the children. When he comes to a river he carries one son across and returns for the other only to see a wolf making off with the first child and a lion with the second.

Now we come to the centrepiece of the painting: here is Eustace (larger than everything else, as was the custom in such pictures), treading water in the middle of the river, hands clasped prayerfully, hoping for better times. The times that come are worse, with the family reunited only to be roasted alive in a brazen bull.

Being in the middle of a river of my own just then, I had a strong fellow-feeling for Eustace. This is where Punch and Judy come into it. Being friends with my head, I was given a little something from my mental archive: seven or eight years earlier I had read in the *New Yorker* magazine two pieces by Edmund Wilson about English Punch and Judy shows and the men who made the puppets and performed with them. ZONK! this freight coupled to the Eustace locomotive and *Riddley Walker* was off down the line on its five-and-a half-year journey to the buffers at Guy Fawkes day, 1979.

Michelangelo is quoted as saying that he did his *David* and other works simply by carving away everything that wasn't the statue. I began *Riddley Walker* in 1974 and by 1976 I had 500 pages that weren't it. I went back to page one, girded up my typewriter and my critical faculty and started over. It wasn't heavy, it was my brother.

I started *Riddley Walker* in straight English but my characters wouldn't wear it, they insisted on breaking up long words and imposing their own grammar, syntax and pronunciation on their vernacular. The Ardship of Cambry, eyeless and misbegotten, assumed the twisted title of the dignitary of our time; Whitstable became Widders Bell, Herne Bay became Horny Boy and so on. People 'vackt their wayt' when they had to leave a place, which is what Erny Orfing does when he has to 'voat no kynd of fents' (this expresses a vote of no confidence as well as giving the image of the security he feels he lacks) and leave the Eusa folk. The language slows the reader down to Riddley's speed as he takes in

what's happening and so effectively becomes a support-
ing player in the action. Since *Riddley Walker* I can't
spell properly any more, but what the hell.

...

POST-SCRIPTS
A FEW FINAL TIPS

BEWARE OF LYRICS

BLAKE MORRISON, AUTHOR OF *AND WHEN DID YOU LAST SEE YOUR FATHER?*

A friend emailed me a while back to ask for advice. She'd just finished a novel that quoted some lines from famous pop songs and she wondered if I'd any tips for her. I had. Just one. *Don't ever quote lines from pop songs.*

I wish someone had given me that advice when I was writing my last novel, *South of the River*, at the end of which there's a party, with music and dancing. As author you get to play DJ, and the tracks I put on for my characters were a mix of 1960s classics and more recent numbers. Because the songs were there not just for atmosphere but to echo events and themes in the novel, it was important, I felt, to include the words, not just the titles.

Of course I knew that when you quote something by a living writer, or even a not-long-dead one, you need permission. Almost every book carries an acknowledgments page, and among the more personal thank yous – 'to my wife for her unstinting support', etc – there's often a more formal credit to such and such a publisher, gallery or record company for permitting a certain item to be reproduced. Such permissions come at a price, and it's usually the author's duty, not the publisher's, to obtain and pay for them. But I'd restricted myself to just a line or two from a handful of songs and vaguely hoped that was OK or that no one would notice.

My editor, reasonably enough, was more cautious, and at the last minute someone from the publishing house helpfully secured the permissions on my behalf. I still have the invoices. For one line of 'Jumpin' Jack Flash': £500. For one line of Oasis's 'Wonderwall': £535. For one line of 'When I'm Sixty-four': £735. For two lines of 'I Shot the Sheriff' (words and music by Bob Marley, though in my head it was the Eric Clapton version): £1,000. Plus several more, of which only George Michael's 'Fastlove' came in under £200. Plus VAT. Total cost: £4,401.75. A typical advance for a literary novel by a first-time author would barely meet the cost.

My publisher, very decently, agreed to go halves. And I've only myself to blame. But it's an interesting illustration of the power of music publishers. Or of the scary lawyers they employ. The logic of their policy is hard to follow. To reproduce lyrics in a book isn't the equivalent of downloading them, because nothing can be heard: it's up to the reader to supply the music, and it's not unfeasible that he or she might then go out and buy the relevant CD. In effect, quoting lyrics is a form of free advertising. But try telling that to the music industry. At a time when piracy, Spotify and unauthorised downloads are eroding its income, it needs every penny it can get, even if that means fleecing fellow-practitioners.

For biographers, permission fees are even more of a nightmare than for poets or novelists, especially if they reproduce images as well as words. In order to raise funds to cover the copyright and reprographic costs of his marvellous biography of Picasso, John Richardson had to create his own foundation – even then, the third volume was delayed and he made no money from it. Tracking down copyright holders and getting answers from them can be a laborious task. But until the subject has been dead for 70 years (it used be a mere 50), there's no getting round it – even if, as Michael Holroyd says, this means enriching the dead at the expense of the living.

The Society of Authors and the Publishers Association have guidelines on what they call 'fair dealing': with prose, a single extract of up to 400 words or a series of extracts of up to 800 words shouldn't require permission; with poetry, up to 40 lines, provided that doesn't exceed a quarter of the poem's length. But these guidelines are only for the purposes of critical commentary, not for an imaginative work, and as far as the music industry is concerned even a line, no matter how banal, constitutes a 'substantial part' of a song. Quoting six words and five syllables from 'You've Lost that Lovin' Feelin' cost me £300.

It would be hypocritical to get too indignant. Poets and novelists also have a living to make, and if someone wants to anthologise us we expect our agents or publishers to charge permission fees, however modest. At least we used to. The internet is gradually changing all that. Now that consumers expect owt for nowt, the temptation is to put stuff in online journals or on your own website, free of charge. It's arguably a more congenial form of self-promotion than Facebook or Twitter. And, since literature is about breaking down barriers, who wants to be associated with a paywall?

In the long run, such liberality will be self-defeating, though: no fee, no win. If authors aren't paid for their words, writing will become a gentlemanly profession again, with only the rich having the wherewithal to do it full-time. Techno-optimists don't see it that way. For them blogging and internet publishing are democratising – a return to a pre-capitalist world of commonality, the online equivalent of oral culture. But the idea that artists have property rights didn't arrive with the Enclosure Act. It's at least as old as ancient Greece. And though breaching copyright is less of an offence than plagiarism, both are a form of theft – a failure to credit the author for his or her creativity.

So though it pained me to fork out £1,000 for 11 words of 'I Shot the Sheriff' – that's more than £90 a word – I mustn't begrudge the Bob Marley estate. But next time I need songs I'll make them up myself. Or do as the narrator does in my new novel, when he hears U2 coming from his housemate's bedroom – refrain from quoting even a syllable of the lyrics.

GET A DEADLINE

GUARDIAN COLUMNIST CHARLIE BROOKER

People often email me asking for advice on how to break into writing, presumably figuring that if a drooling gum-brain like me can scrape a living witlessly pawing at a keyboard, there's hope for anyone.

I rarely respond, partly because there isn't much advice I can give them (apart from 'Keep writing and someone might notice'), and partly because I suspect they're actually seeking encouragement rather than practical guidance. And I'm a terrible cheerleader. I can't egg you on. I just can't. My heart's not in it. To be brutally honest, I'd prefer you to never achieve anything, ever. What if you create a timeless work of art that benefits all humankind? I'm never going to do that; why should you have all the glory? It's selfish of you to even try. Don't you dare so much as start a blog. Seriously. Don't.

Sometimes people go further, asking for advice on the writing process itself. Here I'm equally unhelpful. I've been writing for a living for around 15 years now and whatever method I practise remains a mystery. It's random. Some days I'll rapidly thump out an article in a steady daze, scarcely aware of my own breath. Other times it's like slowly dragging individual letters of the alphabet from a mire of cold glue. The difference, I think, is the degree of self-awareness. When you're consciously trying to write, the words just don't come out. Every sentence is a creaking struggle, and staring out the window with a vague sense of desperation rapidly becomes a coping strategy. To function efficiently as a writer, 95 per cent of your brain has to teleport off into nowhere, taking its neuroses with it, leaving the confident, playful 5 per cent alone to operate the controls. To put it another way: words are like cockroaches; only once the lights are off do they feel free to scuttle around on the kitchen floor. I'm sure I could think of a more terrible analogy than that given another 100,000 years.

Anyway the trick (which I routinely fail to pull off) is to teleport yourself into that productive trance-state as quickly as possible, thereby minimising procrastination and maximising output. I'm insanely jealous of prolific writers, who must either murder their inner critic and float into a productive reverie with ease, or have been fortunate enough to be born with absolutely zero self-critical reflex to begin with.

As for me, I'm stuck in a loveless relationship with myself, the backseat driver who can't stop tutting and nagging. There's no escape from Me's relentless criticism. Me even knows what I'm thinking, and routinely has a pop at Me for that. 'You're worrying about your obsessive degree of self-criticism again,' whines Me. 'How pathetically solipsistic.' And then it complains about its own bleating tone of voice and starts petulantly kicking the back of the seat, asking if we're there yet.

Some days, when a deadline's looming and my brain's refusing to co-operate, I'm tempted to perform some kind of psychological cleansing ceremony. More than once I've wondered whether I should prepare for the writing process by wishing my inner critic inside a nearby object – a tennis ball, say – which I could then symbolically hurl out of the window before taking a seat at my desk.

It sounds like the kind of thing Paul McKenna would do. He's massively successful and can probably levitate.

But before I can even get round to it, I'm plagued with doubts. How far should I throw it? How hard? If I toss 95 per cent of my personality into the garden, do I have to go and retrieve it later? What if it actually works? What if I wind up utterly dependent, and need to perform this ritual every time I'm called upon to do anything – even something as simple as asking for change in a newsagent's – and before long I'm zealously carting a trolley full of tennis balls everywhere I go, violently hurling one into the distance at the start of every sentence, breath, facial expression or bowel movement, and before I know it I've woken up screaming in my own filth in a hospital bed until the man comes in with the needle to make it all go away again? What if that happens?

Yes, what if? So the tennis ball remains untossed, and those typing fingers move unsurely and slowly until the deadline draws sufficiently near enough to become a palpable threat, a looming iceberg whose ominous proximity transforms whines of self-doubt into cries of abject panic. And eventually the page is filled.

So then. To everyone who has ever emailed to ask me for advice on writing, my answer is: get a deadline. That's all you really need. Forget about luck. Don't fret about talent. Just pay someone larger than you to kick your knees until they fold the wrong way if you don't hand in 800 words by five o'clock. You'll be amazed at what comes out.

...✐

LOVE YOUR STATIONERY

HILARY MANTEL, AUTHOR OF *WOLF HALL*

When narratives fracture, when words fail, I take consolation from the part of my life that always works: the stationery order. The mail-order stationery people supply every need from royal blue Quink to a dazzling variety of portable hard drives.

Their operation is error-free, sleek and timely. In fact, it's more than timely: it's eerie. I have only to call out to my spouse: 'Let's be devils and get bubble wrap,' and a man with a van is pulling up outside. Where I live – in the remote vastness of Woking – the morning post comes at three, my parcels go to the right number but another street, and on one occasion, when a hapless person tried to send me a present, Amazon denied that my address existed.

So this speedy stationery service looks spooky. Maybe they've implanted a chip in my brain, and soon I'll only need to think about my order, and coloured lights will flash at their HQ, and the laden vehicle will be screaming in my direction. I can sit and read the stationery catalogue for hours on end, marking its pages with the very Post-it notes it has previously sold me in 12-pad packs. I often wish I could review it: it's crisp and perfectly achieved, and what it lacks in originality it makes up for in the graceful, coded compression of what it offers the dazzled reader

If you think there's little on offer but paperclips, think again: you can buy biscuits, buckets and bayonet-fitting bulbs. Sometimes I fantasise that all my furniture has been destroyed in a cataclysm, and I have to start again with only the stationery catalogue. My entire house would become an office, which would be an overt recognition of the existing state of affairs. Sustained by a giant jar of Fairtrade instant coffee, I could spend whole days putting up Kwik-Rak shelving and assembling 'modular reception seating' into long, worm-shaped sofas. They don't sell beds – so much for office romance – but who would want to rest if you could spend the night printing out masterpieces at your ergonomic melamine workstation, and weighing them at dawn on a 'solar parcel scale', which takes up to 20 kilos and comes with a three-year warranty?

Writers displace their anxiety on to the tools of the trade. It's better to say that you haven't got the right pencil than to say you can't write, or to blame your computer for losing your chapter than face up to your feeling that it's better lost. It's not just writers who muddle up the tools with the job. The reading public also fetishises the kit.

We have all heard the tale of the author who is asked: 'How do you write?' and answers in an exquisitely modulated Nabokovian-Woolfian-Dostoevskian discourse, only to be floored by the flat supplementary: 'I meant, Mac or PC?' There is persistent confusion between writing and writing things down, a confusion between the workings of the writing mind and the weight of the paper scribbled over. 'How many words do you do per day?' people ask, as if the product unwinds in a flowing, ceaseless stream of uncriticised, unrevised narrative, and as if the difference between good and bad writers is that the good ones have no need to do it again. Almost the opposite is true: the better you are, the more ambitious and exploratory, the more often you will go astray on the way to getting it even approximately halfway right.

So while it's on its way to going right, you take comfort in buying new notebooks. Buying them in foreign cities is a good way of carrying away a souvenir. That said, *le vrai moleskine* and its mythology irritate me. Chatwin, Hemingway: has the earth ever held two greater posers? The magic has surely gone out of the little black tablet now that you can buy it everywhere, and in pastel pink, and even get it from Amazon – if they believe your address exists. The trouble with the Moleskine is that you can't easily pick it apart. This may have its advantages for glamorous itinerants, who tend to be of careless habit and do not have my access to self-assembly beech and maple-effect storage solutions – though, as some cabinets run on castors, I don't see what stopped them filing as they travelled. But surely the whole point of a notebook is to pull it apart, and distribute pieces among your various projects? There is a serious issue here. Perforation is vital – more vital than vodka, more essential to a novel's success than a spellchecker and an agent.

I often sense the disappointment when trusting beginners ask me how to go about it, and I tell them it's all about ring binders. But I can only shake my head and say what I know: comrades, the hard-spined note-book is death to free thought. Pocket-size or desk-size, it drives the narrative in one direction, one only, and its relentless linearity oppresses you, so you seal off your narrative options early.

True, you can cross out. You can have a black page to show for your hour's work. Moleskine's website shows a page from a Sartre novel that is almost all crossing-out. But deletion implies you have gone wrong, whereas perhaps you are not going wrong, just generating material in an order the sense of which has yet to emerge. What you need is not to obliterate errors, but to swap them around a bit; then, often enough, they start to look less like errors than like the wellspring of new hope. For myself, the only way I know how to make a book is to construct it like a collage: a bit of dialogue here, a scrap of narrative, an isolated description of a common object, an elaborate running metaphor that threads between the sequences and holds different narrative lines together.

You must be able to loop back on yourself, and to be able to arrange the elements of which your story consists in an order that is entirely flexible. In the end you must make a decision, but why not postpone it till the last possible point? Because once you have made the commitment, what you have written starts to look right. It gains a brutal ascendancy over you. It's easy to revise sentence by sentence, but very difficult to recognise and accept, at some late stage, that the whole structure of a book went wrong because you let your stationery boss you about.

But these days, you'll say, doesn't everybody write on screen? True, but you can still, by premature decision-making about how you store your text, set up for yourself the equivalent of the hard-spined notebook. Files are not flexible unless their maker is. The good news about the computer is its endless scope for procrastinative fussing. Is this a nice font? Shall I rename all my files? Learn some new software?

At twilight, though, when the day's work is on pause, swivelling in my executive chair (variable seat height and de luxe lumbar support), I never reminisce about dear old WordStar 2000 back in the 1980s. I think instead about other trades I might have pursued, with different and privileged stationery: that pink tape, for instance, that barristers use to tie up their bundles.

Do they still, at the Treasury, use treasury tags? Could I use one? The shades of evening make me mourn lost paper sizes; when did you last see a ream of foolscap? The late author David Hughes once sent me a few sheets, and I'm keeping them carefully, for when I have a long, thin story to write.

... NOTES ...